EARTHRIGHTS

EDUCATION AS IF THE
PLANET REALLY MATTERED

SUE GREIG   GRAHAM PIKE   DAVID SELBY

WWF

Kogan Page

EARTHRIGHTS

EDUCATION AS IF THE
PLANET REALLY MATTERED

SUE GREIG   GRAHAM PIKE   DAVID SELBY

WWF

This book draws on the first year's research of a three year project entitled 'Global Impact', which is being carried out on behalf of WWF United Kingdom by the Centre for Global Education.

Sue Greig and Graham Pike are Research Fellows, David Selby is Director, at the Centre for Global Education, University of York, Heslington, York YO1 5DD.

The book is published to coincide with the publication of the report of the World Commission on Environment and Development and the transmission of BBC/North South Production's TV series 'Only One Earth'.

Co-published in 1987 by
The World Wildlife Fund
and
Kogan Page Ltd, 120 Pentonville Road, London N1 9JN

Reprinted 1989, 1990

Copyright © The World Wildlife Fund, 1987

ISBN 1–85091–453–2 [Kogan Page]
ISBN 1–947613–02–1 [World Wildlife Fund]

Typeset by V & M Graphics Ltd, Aylesbury, Bucks
Printed and bound in Great Britain by
Biddles Ltd, Guildford and King's Lynn

Manuscript typed by: Sue Coward
Design by: Schermuly Design Co.
Cover Photograph: BBC/North South Productions

75% of teachers think that 'developing an understanding that the world is an inter-related, interdependent system of lands and peoples' is very important or crucial in the promotion of a global perspective in education.

46% of teachers indicated that their school had policies or guidelines which feature environmental education.

69% of teachers think that environmental and development education are relevant to their subject areas.

67% of teachers think that the political aspects of development and environmental education are *not* too controversial to be dealt with in the classroom.

88% of primary and secondary school teachers think that the children they teach are *not* too young to develop a global awareness or empathy with people from other lands and cultures.

78% of primary and secondary school teachers think that development and environmental education are central to achieving an understanding of, and active participation in the world today.

65% of primary and secondary teachers would welcome in-service training on ways of incorporating development and environmental issues into their teaching.

From the 'Global Impact' survey (1986) of over 800 primary and secondary school teachers in 21 randomly selected local education authorities throughout the United Kingdom.

… As if the planet mattered

'Like a blue pearl in space' was how the first astronauts to circle the planet described what they saw, and when this spark of colour in an ocean of blackness flashed across our television screens it was an image of beauty and fragility 'as powerful as any idea in history'.

Yet just since yesterday, 30,000 hectares (that is an area about the size of the Isle of Wight) of tropical forest have been destroyed or degraded[1], deserts have advanced by a similar area, 200 million tonnes of top soil have been lost through erosion, one species has become extinct and 100,000 people (nearly half of them children) have died through hunger[2]. The life support systems of our planet are beginning to buckle under the pressure of ever increasing human numbers consuming ever increasing amounts of resources.

The speed with which these changes are happening is hard to comprehend. The world's population has doubled in about the last forty years and is projected to double again by the year 2050[1]. We have used as much coal since World War II as had previously been used in the whole of history[2]. Our survival is threatened as much by the inadequacy of our understanding as by our actions.

Treat the earth well
It was not given to you by
your parents
It was loaned to you by your
children

> Africa is full of lonely peasants; millions of people alienated from one another by the destruction of nature … Forests recede day after day and the peasants walk farther and farther for firewood. As the rivers and springs dry up more often, they walk farther and farther for water. As the land gets degraded, the lonely peasant toils only to harvest less year after year … Lamentation alone does not provide enough insight of the predicament of the lonely peasants. When nature recedes, so do the prospects for their well-being. Those threats that tie the peasants to nature are too deep-rooted: their disruption leaves severe wounds on the health and collective consciousness of the people. The lonely peasant is a grim reminder to the rest of humanity of the ultimate implications of a lonely planet.
> Calestous Juma, Kenyan Journalist

'Never before', writes Jean Houston, 'has the responsibility of the human being for the planetary process been greater. Never before have we gained power of such magnitude over the primordial issues of life and death. The density and intimacy of the global village, along with the stagger-ing consequences of our new knowledge and technologies make us directors of a world that up to now has mostly directed us. This is a responsibility for which we have been ill-prepared and for which the usual formulas and stop gap solutions will not work'[3].

In the West our understanding of the world has been largely shaped through science which, until this century, has sought to understand the world by dissecting it, bit by bit. But this approach leaves unanswered the question of how the parts interact to sustain life and evolve. A shift in perspective is now occurring in many disciplines towards a focus on whole systems instead of constituent parts. A system, whether it is a human family or a tropical rainforest, can only be understood by looking at the *relationships* between the individual elements; that is the constant flow of energy, matter or information through the system.

> *We are whirlpools in a river of everflowing water; we are not stuff that abides, but patterns that perpetuate ourselves.*
> Norbert Weiner

Virtually all the elements that make up our bodies are replaced completely every few years and yet we remain recognizable as individuals with a unique personality and store of experiences, that is until the flow of energy and matter through our bodies ceases[4]. In the same way all forms of life are caught up in the cycling of energy and nutrients from the sun, water, air and earth.

When you bite into a hamburger you may be eating nutrients from the grass of the plains of Central America and thereby using resources which were once stored in the rich canopy of the rainforest. In contributing to deforestation in this way you are linked to climatic changes which may have effects on the other side of the globe and to increased erosion which may before long lead to the silting up of the Panama Canal!

Chernobyl

Chernobyl did happen here
'... the Chernobyl accident could not happen here'
Lord Marshall, CEGB Chairman, *Power News*, Sept. 1986.

On 26 April 1986 the nuclear reactor at Chernobyl suffered a major explosion. Although the accident happened 2000 miles away from the United Kingdom, within days a huge cloud of radioactivity was distributed over most of Northern Europe, and British people were being cautioned about drinking fresh rainwater; a frighteningly effective demonstration of global interdependence. Estimates of the long-term health effects range from 8000 additional cancers (Swedish Radiological Protection Board) to 100,000 (Political Ecology Research Group U.K.). Here in the United Kingdom we received far less radioactive fallout than, for example, Sweden,

Poland and West Germany. Even so the extra radiation dose received by those living in the north of Britain is estimated at 15% above normal over the 12 months since the accident, and for those in the south, 1% above normal. All the evidence suggests that there is no threshold level below which there are no additional risks; any increase in exposure increases the probability of cancers and genetic defects. On these figures 140 additional fatal and non-fatal cancers are predicted.

Due to heavy rainfall in upland areas of Britain on 2/3 May there was wet deposition of radioactive fallout on to vegetation in these areas. Consequently the upland sheep farmers of North Wales, Cumbria and South-West Scotland have been particularly affected by the accident. Although the levels of radioactive Iodine decrease relatively quickly, Caesium 137 will still be at half strength 30 years from now. On June 20, 1986, nearly two months after the accident, high levels of radioactivity were recorded in lambs in these upland areas. The highest levels were over four times the intervention limit of 1000 bq kg^{-1} (in Sweden the intervention limit is set lower at 300 bq kg^{-1}). Restrictions were placed on the movement and slaughter of lambs; in Wales alone 2 million sheep on 5100 holdings were affected. In late August 1986, a mark and release scheme was introduced with contaminated sheep being marked with blue paint and being sold at knock-down prices to lowland farmers, who took a gamble that contamination levels would fall and they could then sell the lambs at a profit before the winter. At the end of January 1987, there were still 100,000 sheep under 'farm-arrest' in Wales and

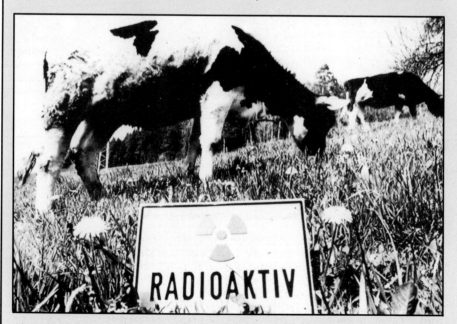

continued

the government had paid in excess of £2.1 million to farmers under various compensation schemes. Although it was suggested by, for example, the Scottish Office, that the biological half-life of Caesium 137 might be 50 days or less, six months after the accident contamination levels of over four times the intervention limit were still being recorded in some Welsh lambs. There is evidence that Caesium 137 can be reabsorbed from the vegetation. The University of Bangor experimented by putting 'clean' sheep on the hills during October, 1986; after four weeks grazing contamination levels of three times the intervention limit were recorded. This indicates that the re-imposition of restrictions on movement and slaughter of sheep in summer 1987 is a possibility and so the damage to the livelihoods of these upland farmers continues.

The Sami of Northern Norway, Finland and Sweden have daily a very tangible reminder of Chernobyl in the reindeer on which their livelihoods depend. Reindeer feed on lichen which is highly sensitive to air pollution. When the first 1000 reindeer were slaughtered during the annual autumn round up, five months after the accident, 97% of carcasses had radiation levels over thirty times Sweden's permissible limit for human consumption. As a result the Scandinavian governments have been urging the Sami to slaughter up to 80% of their reindeer instead of the usual 35%. The governments plan to buy the contaminated meat and feed it to mink and foxes in their fur farms. Several thousand sheep and 17,000 reindeer had already been slaughtered in Norway, at a cost of £21 million, because they contained excessive doses of radiation. The lichens in Northern Scandinavia will continue to pose a hazard for at least 10 years, and meanwhile fish in the area have also been declared unfit to eat. The Sami now face an impossible choice; they must either destroy the reindeer on which their way of life depends or ignore health warnings and eat contaminated meat.

Sources: Collier, J. G. and Davies, L. M. 'Chernobyl' C.E.G.B., 1986: O'Riordan, M. C. and Fry, F. A. 'Cloud over Britain' transcript of talk given at the 1986 meeting of the British Association for the Advancement of Science in Bristol: Fry, F. A., Clarke, R. H. and O'Riordan, M. C. 'Early estimates of U.K. radiation doses from the Chernobyl reactor' Nature Vol. 321, 1986: Sunday Times Magazine, Nov. 30, 1986 and March 15, 1987.

We live in a seamless world where local is but one point in the web at which all disturbances in the whole are unavoidably felt.

Whatever befalls the earth befalls the sons of the earth. If men spit upon the ground, they spit on themselves. This we know – the earth does not belong to man, man belongs to the earth. All things are connected like the blood which unites one family. Whatever befalls the earth befalls the sons of the earth. Man did not weave the web of life; he is merely a strand in it. Whatever he does to the web he does to himself.

Chief Seattle, 1855

It may seem like a truism then to say that the condition of our lives, indeed our survival, and the state of the global environment are interdependent and yet our lifestyles tend to numb us to this most intimate of connections. Our interrelatedness is often only translated into a reality when some part of the system is at crisis point, and then only when the costs are felt in our pockets or in our state of health.

Even measured in narrow economic terms, the costs of environmental damage are extremely high and continually rising. For example, acid rain, which is now affecting an area in Europe equivalent to that of the U.K., is estimated to cost West Germany alone $2.8 billion per year. Soil erosion is estimated to cost the U.S.A. $6 billion per year in lost agricultural production. In developing countries of the South the environmental crisis is deeper and more immediate since a greater share of their economies depends directly on natural resources. Soil erosion in Ethiopia, which has resulted from a decline in forest cover from 25% to 3% since 1940, cuts agricultural output by at least one million tonnes of food per year, equivalent to two thirds of food relief shipped in 1985[5]. It has been suggested that, where the environment is concerned, we are failing to distinguish between capital and income earned from the capital. As Fritz Schumacher points out 'every economist and businessman is familiar with the distinction and applies it conscientiously and with considerable subtlety to all economic affairs – except where it really matters: namely the irreplaceable capital which man has not made, but simply found, and without which he can do nothing'[6].

There have been many international commissions and conferences which have concluded with roughly the same message: 'if present trends continue, the world in 2000 will be more crowded, more polluted, less stable ecologically and more vulnerable to disruption. Despite greater material output, the world's people will be poorer in many ways than they are today'[7].

What then are the barriers to a more sustainable, rational use of global resources? This is clearly a hugely complex question but part of the problem lies in our lifestyles and patterns of consumption. In the rich countries of the North we (25% of the world's population) consume roughly 80% of the world's resources, leaving 20% to be divided up by the remaining 75% of the world's people. In the United Kingdom we eat on average three times as much and consume forty times the amount of fossil fuels as the average citizen in the 'Third World'[8]. Our consumption patterns are not only excessive, but also extremely wasteful, being geared to resource depletion rather than conservation. The United Kingdom alone produces a total of 23 million tonnes of rubbish every year, much of which is just buried in landfills[9]. When measured in terms of the relative ecological burden it is clear that population control or limiting of consumption in the North is more of a priority than population control in the South.

Rubbish!

Each household in the U.K. produces on average 1 tonne of rubbish per year; a third of this is packaging and about a tenth is food. As a nation we produce a total of 23 million tonnes of rubbish a year. Let's take paper: 7 million tonnes are currently used per year worldwide, of which about 30% is recycled. It is estimated that if just 50% were recycled 8 million hectares of forest would be saved. The recycling of glass is particularly costly in energy terms and therefore re-use is a more efficient policy (milk bottles are re-used 8-25 times). However the number of returnable bottles has continued to decrease. We use annually 6 billion disposable glass containers, of which only a tiny fraction find their way into bottle banks. Bottle banks in Leeds collected a paltry 5 bottles per year for each person in the city. In one area of Paris special containers designed to avoid breakage are in use; wine bottles of different kinds are then sorted automatically and the scheme aims to return 12,000 tons of bottles into use each year. Several states in the U.S. have passed legislation which ensures that all beverage containers should carry deposits and be returnable; Friends of the Earth have been campaigning for similar legislation in the U.K. so far without success.

The story in the developing world is different in that the economy in these countries is, of necessity, geared to resource conservation. Rubbish tips in developing countries are often an important source of raw materials and are sites of intense entrepreneurial activity. In many capital cities, hundreds of people literally live on rubbish dumps, frequently in such squalor that they suffer substantially reduced life expectancy as a result. In India scrap collectors may be killed or maimed during their hunt for spent cartridge cases on army firing ranges.

However, there are some imaginative schemes which aim to both save energy and provide employment. In one Latin American town a cooperative took over the concession for salvage at the local dump, which had been previously held by the mafia. After five years the average income per family had increased from $4 to $50 per week. The co-operative also now runs medical and educational programmes, and employs a full-time health worker. In the Philippines the *Pera Sa Basura* project aims to make Manila the 'cleanest city in Asia'. It began with a campaign to persuade slum-dwellers to separate wet and dry rubbish. 'Redemption centres' have also been opened where recyclables are brought, then sold to boost community funds. The collection of rubbish is done by former scavengers, now transformed into 'Eco-Aides' with equipment, protective clothing and guaranteed prices for what they salvage. Manila also has a thriving glass-recycling system; some people work the streets buying empty bottles, others work as bottle sorters or bottle washers. The clean bottles are sold to local soft-drinks firms and the local fish-sauce industry, and any breakages go into the cullet bin to be sold to a glass manufacturer.

Rubbish at Everest basecamp in Nepal

Sources: *New Internationalist No. 114, 1982 and No. 157, 1986: Earth Resources Research 'Waste Recycling' Information Sheet 5: Gaia Atlas of Planet Management, Pan Books, 1985.*

It is also now very arguable whether this level of overconsumption has brought a corresponding increase in well-being. The loss of the 'natural' environment is keenly felt and we seek out those remaining corners of wilderness for enjoyment and relaxation, but also for a deeper sustenance. In her book, Nor Hall eloquently argues the need for a spiritual re-connection which recognises our interdependence with the earth and its natural resources:

'... the soul-felt, *necessary* enactments of the interrelationship between human beings and the green-life, rock-life, animal-life and planet-life. We are coming to a point in our habitation of earth where these rituals respecting nature are necessary. (We need ways to recognize collectively the spiritual dimension to water cycles and fuel cycles, for example – ways to recognize our essential dependence.) Is there a way to re-enact the fact that man is as much dependent upon and part of the fossil fuel he burns as the primitive hunter was dependent upon and part of the deer he ate? Ancient fears of physical survival are coming up again out of necessity to balance the very great fears of psychic survival that characterize our time'[10].

The stresses and strains which these patterns of consumption place on the environment are mirrored in our bodies. Heart complaints, mental breakdowns, certain types of cancer are just some of the ailments which have been linked to our 'prosperous' lifestyle.

However, the human problems of the global affluent minority pale into insignificance when compared with those of the majority of the world's people. According to the World Bank nearly half the people alive today live in relative or absolute poverty. Absolute poverty is defined as 'a condition of life so characterised by malnutrition, illiteracy and disease as to be beneath any reasonable definition of human decency' and this is the nature of existence for 800 million people with whom we share the globe.

The main environmental concern for the people of the South is not the quality of life but life itself. It is the poor of the developing countries who are most affected by environmental degradation, and at the same time they are often forced by circumstance to destroy the very resources on which they depend.

Everyone has the right to a standard of living adequate for the health and well-being of himself and of his family, including food, clothing, housing and medical care and necessary social services.
Universal Declaration of Human Rights, 1948, Article 25.1

The metaphor of eating the seed corn for next year's planting is duplicated time after time throughout the Third World. There can be no clearer demonstration that those who are working for a better environment must simultaneously devote themselves to working for social justice. There is not only the moral imperative which compels us to seek ways of sharing the world's wealth more effectively; there is the ecological imperative to remind us that the protection of the Earth's natural systems is something we all depend on.
Jonathon Porritt, *Seeing Green*

The perpetuation of poverty and despair amongst the majority of the world's population constitutes a denial of human rights on an immense scale and leads inevitably to increasing social tensions and conflict. The gaps in material wealth both between and within societies are widening. Between 1950 and 1980 real per capita income for the 800 million people in the world's poorest countries grew by a mere $80. Over the same period in the industrialised countries it rose by $6,000[11]. This widening gap between the haves and the have-nots is also apparent in the United Kingdom; unemployment rates have doubled since 1980 and for those in work the gap in earnings between manual and non-manual workers has widened over the same period[12]. These glaring differences are made all the more visible by the rich world's communications systems.

What is happening is that [the poor] see their poverty ... with much sharper eyes. Before they tolerated it; today they say 'Why should we tolerate it?'

Indira Gandhi

The same technology which has made possible such an explosion in the use of natural resources has created weapons of unprecedented destruction. The arms race consumes resources at an enormous rate; world military expenditures are over $1 million every minute, more than 30 times greater than the net transfer of financial resources from rich to poor countries[13]. If just eight hours of military spending, worth $680 million, could be diverted, we might eradicate malaria, a debilitating disease from which 200 million people worldwide suffer[2]. Two-thirds of the arms trade is conducted between developed and developing countries[14]. In 1980 the per capita military expenditure in developing countries was nearly three times the per capita expenditure on health[13], and this at a time when 44% of the population did not have access to safe drinking water. Nearly half of these countries are under military control, and have a record of human rights violations, including torture, brutality, 'disappearances' and political killings[13].

'Oxfam News' June 85

The arms race is a significant factor in the widening gap between the rich and the poor, not only in terms of resource consumption, but also in the distorting effect it has on the growth of science and technology. A fifth of the world's scientists and engineers were engaged in military work in the 1970s. In 1980 the global expenditures on military research and development were approximately $35 billion, or a quarter of all research spending, which is, it is claimed, more than the total amount spent on energy, health, pollution control and agriculture[15].

Most significantly, the arms race helps to create the very conditions of increasing tension and instability which make the use of nuclear weapons much more likely.

> *Development strategies biased against the poor create the conditions that generate popular opposition, which in turn breeds violence and repression from those in power. The military and paramilitary forces step in at this stage, and in the process increase their share of the domestic budget and external aid. This further squeezes social expenditures and increases discontent.*
>
> Gita Sen & Caren Grown[16]

Our consumption patterns in the richer countries of the North are a double-edged sword, at once cushioning us from global resource depletion and degradation and the human misery with which it is inextricably linked, whilst at the same time accelerating the process. The lifestyles 'enjoyed' today by an affluent minority are sustained at great cost to the global environment and the disadvantaged majority of the world's population. There are those who believe that more advanced technology will provide the answer, but science and technology do not operate in a vacuum. As Ronald Higgins reminds us, 'it is human choice that decides how technologies are applied and political conditions that largely determine their social impact. Those who rise in spasms of hope that processed plankton or high-yielding seeds will resolve the food crisis have forgotten the brutal truth that the poor have no money to pay for them and the crueller truth that innovation often just makes the rich richer, the fat fatter'[17].

For women there are no developed countries

Women are half of the world's population, a third of the official labour force, and do two-thirds of the world's work. Yet they earn one-tenth of its income and own one-hundredth of its property.

'Economic development is often still talked about as if it was mainly a subject for men. Plans and projects are designed by men to be implemented by men ... Thus women remain ... invisible. Yet their contributions are indispensible and basic.' *Brandt Report*

In one village in Burkina Faso solar cookers were introduced in an effort to save fuel-gathering time; they were designed and mostly made in Denmark and the women of the village neither asked for them, nor were they consulted. They are not much used because most cooking is done after sunset, the structure needs resetting every 15 minutes to follow the sun, they only take a small pot which has to be made of metal and it is difficult to cook common foods on the flimsy structure because they require vigorous stirring.

The women of developing countries are often the most vociferous in the struggle against environmental degradation; it is they who have to walk further and further as a result to collect the water, firewood or food which their families need.

'Poverty is the worst form of environmental pollution in developing countries. This poverty is something that many men can run away from – admittedly often into worse poverty in the cities – while the woman and her children are left behind in the country. It is she who has to worry about how to feed her family, what to cook with, where she will get water from, why the topsoil is being lost, how she will grow enough food. What the National Council of Women of Kenya does is campaign; it tells people why they should plant trees, and they have responded very well ... These trees are planted as a community woodland which we call a "green belt" ... I think the tree growing project has been so successful because the people can see the crisis – there are not enough trees and not enough firewood.' *Wangari Maathai*

continued

'The woman who works on a farm may provide everything for her family but it is not recognised because the product is eaten. Men then have time for building huts, planting, hunting and local wage labour. These earnings are spent on themselves, on things like bikes and alcohol. The men feel they own the things they have produced. What the woman has produced has gone.' *Buchi Emecheta*

Buchi Emecheta writes of African women yet what she says is true, in essence, for women the world over. Women are marginalised by social, political and economic structures worldwide. A sexual division of labour exists which allocates women to the most onerous, labour intensive, poorly rewarded tasks both inside and outside the home, as well as to the longest hours of work. In the industrialised world a housewife does on average 56 hours unpaid work per week, the one in three women who have jobs do 31 hours unpaid work and this compares with the 11 hours unpaid work done on average by a man with a job. It is estimated that in industrialised countries unpaid housework contributes between 25% and 40% of the Gross National Product.

The women's movement has begun to challenge the accepted values of the world. Women have come together to tackle problems of income, of employment, of health and of childcare. Women throughout the world are campaigning for the environment, for equality and for peace. Central to the women's movement is a reassertion of the emotional and spiritual dimensions of human existence and a redefinition of power. In Stephanie Leland's words 'many of us have experienced the sense of power we have as women through the regeneration of shared energy, the understanding that we are not alone, and the belief that together we have the power to act – to effect change'. Women are speaking with a uniquely powerful and hopeful voice for the continuance of life on earth.

Sources: 'Our Own Freedom' Maggie Murray and Buchi Emecheta 1981: 'Reclaim the Earth' Leonie Caldecott and Stephanie Leland (eds.) 1983: 'Women – A World Report' New Internationalist, 1985.

In Meadows' words 'a whole culture has evolved around the principle of fighting against limits, rather than learning to live with them'[18], and in this context technology has achieved a momentum all of its own.

Western society has accepted as unquestionable a technological imperative that is quite as arbitrary as the most primitive taboo: not merely the duty to foster invention and constantly to create technological novelties, but equally the duty to surrender to these novelties unconditionally, just because they are offered, without respect to their human consequences.

Lewis Mumford

The relationships between technology and development processes are undoubtedly complex but there is considerable evidence that the wholesale transfer of industrial advanced technology to developing countries has been associated with increased inequality and environmental degradation[19]. The deleterious effects of such transfers are also exacerbated by frequent abandonment of controls, which are legally required in the North, to reduce pollution or health hazards.

Many scientific studies have shown that the basic issue is not lack of resources but one of their distribution and the use to which they are put. The entire planet's population can be adequately housed and fed and enjoy a livelihood which allows them to live beyond the fear of poverty[2]. We need to find pathways (social, political, economic and technological) to development which is within the 'inner limits' of basic human needs and the 'outer limits' of the planet's physical resources; i.e. a redefinition of the notion of development is required.

How can the spirit of the earth like the White man? ...
Everywhere the White man has touched it, it is sore.
a Wintu (Native American) woman

The idea of development is based on a metaphor of unfolding or unrolling, as in the root meaning of the word. Under the pressures of the dominant system this has been interpreted as the working through of an inherent set of processes or priorities. To fail to share these is to be 'undeveloped' or 'underdeveloped'. But these processes do not come from inside some metaphysical or world-historical roll, which history merely unfolds. They are all positively instituted, by identifiable interests and with identifiable results. To assess, to review, to monitor, to choose among these processes and priorities is then, in a modern sense, to develop 'development' itself.

Raymond Williams

In seeking ways towards sustainable development perhaps we should be prepared more often to, in Michael Redclift's words, 'take our cues from societies whose very existence "development" has always threatened'[19].

The Chinese character 'ji' means at once crisis and opportunity; and throughout the world opportunities for new ways of thinking and acting are being seized. Research and development work *is* being done to find appropriate or alternative technologies. Economists are looking at ways of taking environmental costs into account, instead of writing them off as by-products or side-effects, somehow 'external' to the production process. At an international level the need to take an holistic view of world problems is

recognised in the publications of the Brandt Commission, *North–South*[20] and *Common Crisis*[21], and also in the *World Conservation Strategy*[22]. In 1983 the United Nations set up the Brundtland Commission to 'look ahead at critical environmental and development problems and propose better ways and means for the world community to address them'[23].

The world is shrinking rapidly. We share a world economy; a world environment, which is the basis for the present and future world economy; and a stake in world development and a decent, dignified human condition of life. We must learn to think globally and in a long-term perspective.

Gro Harlem Brundtland

At a local level many initiatives have been characterised by an identification with collective rather than self-interest, combined with a commitment to, and belief in, personal action. Community self-help schemes throughout the world testify to the effectiveness of this 'bottom up' approach in finding appropriate and sustainable solutions (see pages 8-15). Nor have such local groups failed to make wider connections, many forming networks in which the commonality and interdependence of their aims and hopes are recognised. Such networks are voluntary associations which derive their binding force from a deep personal commitment to a few basic assumptions shared by all[24]. Through such networks information, resources, insight and encouragement flow, much facilitated by the speed and sophistication of present-day communications. Networks are self-organising and, as such, quite unlike traditional political structures; they overlap, form coalitions and support each other without generating a conventional power structure. There are environmental groups, women's groups, human rights groups, peace groups; groups campaigning for an end to world hunger, all organised in this way. Their potential for change lies in the combination of local action with the global cohesion afforded by the network.

Tree-hugging

The Chipko Andolan movement in northern India grew out of a realisation by local people that the heavy flooding, soil erosion and landslides they had suffered, with the loss of many lives, were linked to the extent of deforestation. In the area, forest wealth is distributed by auction, but the local community was unable to compete with powerful business interests.

Their campaign for the restoration of local control of the forests met with no success, and when a contract to remove trees, required locally for making agricultural implements, was awarded to a manufacturer of sports goods, they decided to resist further loss by hugging the trees and daring the company contractors to let the axe fall on their backs. This threat was successful for a time, but then, when all the men of the local villages were away, the contractors took the opportunity to move into the forest.

They had, however, reckoned without the local women. A group, who daily went into the forest to collect fuel and medicinal herbs, tried to persuade the lumbermen to stop. One woman was threatened with a gun and she responded by telling the man to shoot because 'then only can you cut this forest which is like a mother to us'. The lumbermen, unnerved by this confrontation with supposedly passive and reticent Hindu women, retreated. The women then succeeded in dislodging a large concrete slab

continued

which had been keeping a narrow section of the road to the forest passable (landslides had destroyed the original track). The road to the forest was closed. Two years later a scientific inquiry concluded that the region's slopes were at a critical threshold of stability and all tree-felling in the area was banned for a ten year period.

The Chipko workers have continued to work for forest preservation, through education and reforestation programmes, and in this way to fight for environmentally-sensitive and therefore sustainable development in the Himalaya. Their philosophy advocates self-rule on a personal level and opposes the centralisation of leadership, except leadership by example. The Chipko action of bargaining for a tree's life with one's own is in the classic Ghandhian tradition of non-violent protest, a tradition deeply rooted in the Hindu belief in, and respect for, the essential unity of life and nature. The Chipko movement has been described as the developing world's first environmentalist movement which has liberated itself from the constraints of the western worldview.

Source: *Haigh, M. 'The Chipko Movement' in Reclaiming the Earth: Development and the Environment 'Links 19' Third World First, 1984.*

think globally

act locally

A new vision of the world is emerging; a world in which the whole is more than the sum of the parts, a world in which things exist only in relationship with other things, a world which values differences as well as sameness, a world in which the emotional and the spiritual are as real and as important as the rational, a world in which the ability to create is valued more than the ability to destroy, and a world in which we are not in control of nature but are rooted in it. This new worldview or paradigm resonates within our inner selves and awakens new possibilities.

Through nurturing and exploring those qualities in ourselves which have lain dormant, we can allow the growth of new relationships with ourselves, with each other and with the planet; relationships that are based on trust and respect instead of fear and exploitation. And in so doing we are able to respond positively and creatively to the challenges of our times.

Whatever you may think about yourself, and however long you may have thought it, you are not just you. You are a seed. A silent promise.
Marilyn Ferguson, *The Aquarian Conspiracy*

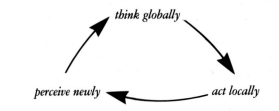

To destroy a hectare of rainforest, lose an inch of topsoil, or for a species to become extinct can take a matter of hours or days, but to replace what has been lost, if indeed that is possible, may take tens or even hundreds of years. We must therefore take a long view and engage with thinking about the future. However there is a danger that, in Jonathon Porritt's words, 'the poor haven't the luxury and the rich haven't the inclination to think about tomorrow'[18]. This lack of inclination may not be indicative of indifference; it can stem at one level from ignorance or incomprehension of the complexity of the interdependent world in which we live, and at another from fear of acknowledging the dangers which face us. This fear leads to apathy (literally, the inability or the refusal to feel pain) and a sense of helplessness[25].

In education, perhaps more than in any other sphere of human activity, looking to the future, and with hope rather than despair, is of vital importance. It is also something which the citizens of the twenty-first century have a right to expect.

> *I owe an allegiance to the planet that has made me possible, and to all the life on that planet, whether friendly or not. I also owe an allegiance to the 3½ billion years of life that made it possible for me to be here, and all the rest of you too. We have a responsibility to the largest population of all, the hundred of billions of people who have not yet been born, who have a right to be, who deserve a world at least as beautiful as ours, whose genes are now in our custody and no one else's.*

David Brower, Chairperson, Friends of the Earth

A Parable

Once upon a time there was a class
and the students expressed disapproval of their teacher.
Why should they be concerned with
global interdependency, global problems
and what others of the world were thinking, feeling and doing?
And the teacher said she had a dream in which she
saw one of her students fifty years from today.
The student was angry and said,

continued

'Why did I learn so much detail about the past
and the administration of my country
and so little about the world?'
He was angry because no one told him
that as an adult he would be faced
almost daily with problems of a
global interdependent nature, be they
problems of peace, security, quality
of life, food, inflation, or scarcity
of natural resources.
The angry student found he was the
victim as well as the beneficiary.
'Why was I not warned? Why was
I not better educated? Why
did my teachers not tell me about
the problems and help me understand
I was a member of an interdependent human race?'
With even greater anger the student shouted,
'You helped me extend my hands with incredible machines,
my eyes with telescopes and microscopes,
my ears with telephones, radios, and sonar,
my brain with computers,
but you did not help me extend
my heart, love, concern
to the entire human family.
You, teacher, gave me half a loaf.'

Jon Rye Kinghorn

Some questions for educators

There is an old Chinese curse which goes 'may you live in interesting times!'. This double-edged blessing gets its delicate irony from the fact that times which are interesting are usually times of upheaval and exceedingly challenging and uncomfortable for the people who live in them. Our fast-changing, interdependent world is certainly amongst the most 'interesting' in human history. Challenges, however, bring opportunities and not least for those responsible for educating subsequent generations.

Other generations believed that they had the luxury of preparing their children to live in a society similar to their own. Ours is the first generation to have achieved the Socratic wisdom of knowing that we do not know the world in which our children will live.

John Goodlad

How should school go about preparing young people for informed and effective participation in world society? How can teachers best help develop global understanding in those who face the exciting yet daunting prospect of adult life in the twenty-first century? What skills, capacities and insights do students need to make sense of, cope with and handle an accelerating rate of change? How can the curriculum as a whole be infused with global and future-facing perspectives? What should the classroom look like as far as teaching and learning styles, climate and relationships are concerned?

A proliferation of 'educations'

Development education, environmental education, human rights education and peace education are four recent initiatives that have addressed the above – and related – questions. Each initiative has tried to influence the education system by setting up teachers' networks, publicising examples of noteworthy practice and making available good classroom resources. In response to this proliferation of 'educations', there have also been important developments aimed at clustering them all under a more inclusive title such as 'world studies' or 'global education'. Such developments recognise the difficulty even the committed teacher has in coming to terms with and implementing so many 'educations', however important she considers each to be. They also recognise that, whilst each 'education' has its own distinctive features and starting points, their concerns are finally mutual and overlapping. Questions concerning the development of human communities and environmental conservation cannot be separated on the world stage, or in the classroom.

Development education

Development education grew out of the mounting concern of charitable organisations, the churches and the United Nations over 'Third World' poverty. This led, particularly in the 1960s and early 1970s, to courses and course units which focussed exclusively upon the plight of chosen 'Third World' countries. From these origins thinking has progressively become much more sophisticated and diversified so that the following perspectives and insights are now all strongly represented in the field:

☐ to understand the level of development in a particular country, the impact of global economic and political systems has also to be studied;

☐ development education is about understanding development processes within and between all countries, rich and poor;

☐ what is appropriate development in one context is not necessarily appropriate in another;

☐ those in the West have much to learn from non-Western perspectives on development;

☐ the 'Third World' is not just a term to describe economically poor nations, but also encompasses areas and groups that have been marginalised by the workings of economic and political systems (e.g. women, the aged, the homeless, the unemployed, ethnic minorities, indigenous peoples, and poor, remote or uninfluential parts of wealthy countries).

The influential Brandt Report, *North–South* (1980), with its emphasis upon the interdependent nature of the contemporary world, did much to help quicken the shift from a narrow to a broad-focus conception of development education. The statement drawn up at the second national conference of the National Association of Development Education Centres (see this page) provides a succinct statement of that broad focus and pinpoints the importance of promoting knowledge, skills and attitudes which will enable individuals better to influence their world.

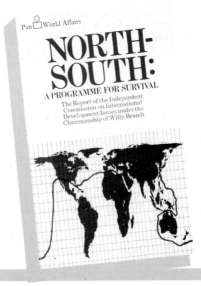

Pan World Affairs

NORTH-SOUTH:
A PROGRAMME FOR SURVIVAL

The Report of the Independent Commission on International Development Issues under the Chairmanship of Willy Brandt

The objective of development education is to enable us to comprehend and participate in the development of ourselves, our community, our nation and the world.
Such 'comprehension' is gained from an educational process engendering understanding and empathy of the cultures, values and ways of life of other people (both of the local community and of other nations), and providing an overview of the power structures, interdependencies and processes which control development of our community, nation and world.
Such 'participation' is facilitated by an educational process which stimulates creativity, the asking of questions and the belief that everyone has a role to play in bringing about change.
Such 'development' implies change for the betterment of the individual, the society within which the individual exists and the world at large. Development education is not more concerned with the individual than with society; not less; they are two sides of the same coin.

NADEC, 1980

Environmental education

In the United Kingdom, the term 'environmental education' was first coined in 1965. It, too, has both a narrow and broad focus. Teachers at the narrow focus have tended to concentrate their teaching upon the local environment, natural and human-made, or upon the purely biological or geographical aspects of environmental study. The call for a much more holistic and biopolitical approach was made at the U.N. Intergovernmental Conference on Environmental Education in Tbilisi, U.S.S.R., in 1977 (see this page) and, again, when the World Wildlife Fund, the United Nations Environment Programme and the International Union for the Conservation of Nature and Natural Resources jointly launched the *World Conservation Strategy* in 1980. The *Strategy*, which appeared hard on the heels of the Brandt Report, underlined the interdependent nature of all components of the biosphere, including human communities, and thus directly linked the future of the planet's life-support systems to human behaviour and development decisions. 'A new ethic, embracing plants and animals as well as people is required for human societies to live in harmony with the natural world on which they depend for survival and well-being,' the *Strategy* urged. 'The long term task of environmental education is to foster or reinforce attitudes and behaviour compatible with this new ethic.'

The goals of environmental education
(a) to foster clear awareness of, and concern about, economic, social, political and ecological interdependence in urban and rural areas;
(b) to provide every person with opportunities to acquire the knowledge, values, attitudes, commitment and skills needed to protect and improve the environment;
(c) to create new patterns of behaviour of individuals, groups and society as a whole towards the environment.
Tbilisi Recommendations, 1980

What the Brandt Report did for development education, the *World Conservation Strategy* has done for environmental education. In the 1980s teaching and learning about the environment is increasingly marked by:

☐ a recognition that the local environment is caught up in the global ecosystem;

☐ an awareness that human and natural systems interact in myriad ways and that there is no part of human activity which does not have a bearing on the environment and vice versa;

☐ a dawning acknowledgement of how much we can learn from other cultures and, perhaps especially, indigeneous peoples, about how to relate to the environment;

☐ an emphasis on the development of environment-friendly values, attitudes and skills (including, very importantly, those skills appropriate to influencing public opinion and political decision making).

All European tradition, Marxism included, has conspired to defy the natural order of things. Mother Earth has been abused, the powers have been abused, and this cannot go on forever. No theory can alter that simple fact. Mother Earth will retaliate, and the abusers will be eliminated. Things come full circle, back to where they started. That's revolution.

American Indians have been trying to explain this to Europeans for centuries. But, as I said earlier, Europeans have proven themselves unable to hear. The natural order will win out, and the offenders will die out, the way deer die out when they offend the harmony by overpopulating a given region. It's only a matter of time until what Europeans call 'a major catastrophe of global proportions' will occur. It is the role of American Indian peoples, the role of all natural beings, to survive. A part of our survival is to resist. We resist not to overthrow a government or to take political power, but because it is natural to resist extermination, to survive. We don't want power over white institutions; we want white institutions to disappear. That's *revolution.*

Russell Means, member of the Oglala Lakota tribe

Human rights education

Human rights education has long enjoyed high-level support from international organisations, such as the United Nations and the Council of Europe, but only recently has that support begun to be translated into good practice undertaken by real teachers with real students in real schools.

In the Third World, the basic human rights are survival and liberation ... following these rights come the right to cultural integrity after years of colonial occupation.... There must be some way, demand the people of the Third World, to prioritize human rights so as to distinguish rights of necessity from rights of preference. Giving priority to rights of survival and liberation may be the first step toward resolving the enormous disparities among the three worlds[26].

The teaching of human rights in the United Kingdom has often adopted a narrow focus. *Civil and political rights* (i.e. individual freedoms such as freedom of speech and freedom of movement) have been the main object of study with relatively little attention given to *social and economic rights* (i.e. those that ensure material and bodily well-being, such as the right to food and shelter). There has also been a rather uncritical acceptance of Western individual-istic notions of rights and some reluctance to stray beyond those laid down in key international documents such as the *Universal Declaration of Human Rights* (1948). Those teaching to a narrow rights focus have insufficiently recognised that *new rights, reflecting new human pre-occupations, need constantly to be identified.* Broad focus rights educators, on the other hand, have shown a preparedness to broaden their teaching to include non-Western concepts of rights and new rights issues that have emerged subsequent to the major international docu-ments, such as racism, sexism, the right to development and the rights implications of environmental abuse.

The understanding and experience of human rights is an important element in the preparation of all young people for life in a democratic and pluralistic society. It is part of social and political education, and it involves intercultural and international understanding.

Recommendation of the Committee of Ministers to Member States on Teaching and Learning about Human Rights in Schools, Council of Europe, 1985. The British government was a signatory.

Peace education

The original 1960s' focus of concern of peace education – with the horrors of the Second World War not long past and the arms race in full swing – was studying war and disarmament. Teachers also looked for ways in which schools could help create more positive attitudes to the peoples of other nations and so foster international understanding. Since the 1960s, the focus has broadened to include not only *negative peace* (i.e. absence of war) but also *positive peace* (i.e. ways of creating more just structures in and between societies). A society or world characterised by injustice, oppression and exploitation may seem superficially peaceful in the absence of actual physical violence but a 'masked violence is constantly done to the rights and lives of human beings'[27]. Broad-focus peace educators in the 1980s would, therefore, include questions of violence/non-violence, poverty/economic welfare and injustice/justice within their working definition. They would also embrace the study of conflict, conflict avoidance and resolution between individuals, groups and nations. Finally, they would want to explore the question of humanity's relationship with the environment and encourage their students to consider whether and in what ways we need to modify our behaviours, expectations and values so as to bring greater harmony (peacefulness) to that relationship.

Four educations? One education?

Interestingly, the four 'educations' share relatively few and sometimes no mutual or overlapping concerns at their narrow focus (see fig. 1). A purely local or biological approach to environmental education, for instance, has little or nothing in common with studying poverty in the 'Third World' (narrow focus development education) or

Figure 1

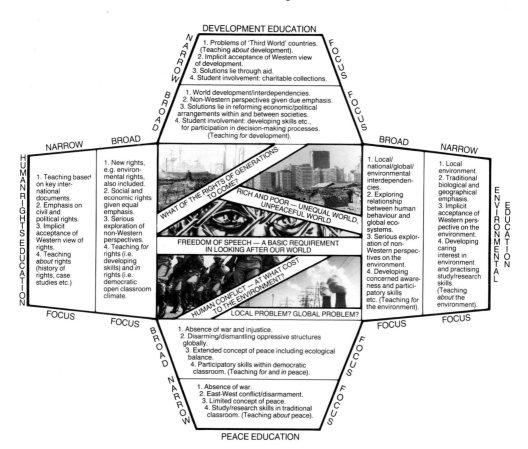

DEVELOPMENT EDUCATION

NARROW FOCUS
1. Problems of 'Third World' countries. (Teaching *about* development).
2. Implicit acceptance of Western view of development.
3. Solutions lie through aid.
4. Student involvement: charitable collections.

BROAD FOCUS
1. World development/interdependencies.
2. Non-Western perspectives given due emphasis.
3. Solutions lie in reforming economic/political arrangements within and between societies.
4. Student involvement: developing skills etc., for participation in decision-making processes. (Teaching *for* development).

HUMAN RIGHTS EDUCATION

NARROW FOCUS
1. Teaching based on key international documents.
2. Emphasis on civil and political rights.
3. Implicit acceptance of Western view of rights.
4. Teaching *about* rights (history of rights, case studies etc.)

BROAD FOCUS
1. New rights, e.g. environmental rights, also included.
2. Social and economic rights given equal emphasis.
3. Serious exploration of non-Western perspectives.
4. Teaching *for* rights (i.e. developing skills) and *in* rights (i.e. democratic open classroom climate.

WHAT OF THE RIGHTS OF GENERATIONS TO COME?

RICH AND POOR — UNEQUAL WORLD, UNPEACEFUL WORLD

FREEDOM OF SPEECH — A BASIC REQUIREMENT IN LOOKING AFTER OUR WORLD

HUMAN CONFLICT — AT WHAT COST TO THE ENVIRONMENT?

LOCAL PROBLEM? GLOBAL PROBLEM?

ENVIRONMENTAL EDUCATION

BROAD FOCUS
1. Local/ national/global/ environmental interdependencies.
2. Exploring relationship between human behaviour and global ecosystems.
3. Serious exploration of non-Western perspectives on the environment.
4. Developing concerned awareness and participatory skills etc. (Teaching *for* the environment).

NARROW FOCUS
1. Local environment.
2. Traditional biological and geographical emphasis.
3. Implicit acceptance of Western perspective on the environment.
4. Developing caring interest in environment and practising study/research skills. (Teaching *about* the environment).

PEACE EDUCATION

BROAD FOCUS
1. Absence of war and injustice.
2. Disarming/dismantling oppressive structures globally.
3. Extended concept of peace including ecological balance.
4. Participatory skills within democratic classroom. (Teaching *for* and *in* peace).

NARROW FOCUS
1. Absence of war.
2. East-West conflict/disarmament.
3. Limited concept of peace.
4. Study/research skills in traditional classroom. (Teaching *about* peace).

with studying war and disarmament (narrow focus peace education). At their broad focus, however, there is an extremely marked degree of convergence between the four 'educations' to the point where it becomes difficult to conceive of them as discrete fields. Why is this?

1. *Those working at the broad focus have come to recognize that their respective principal concepts – development, environment, human rights and peace – are complementary, interdependent and mutually illuminating.*

For instance:

☐ development decisions for human communities cannot disregard their environmental impact without, in the short or long term, jeopardising human development;

☐ environmental conservation is not contrary to development but an essential consideration if we are to work to create human lifestyles that are sustainable;

☐ development is essentially about the realisation of material and non-material human rights just as undevelopment or distorted development and their effects – malnutrition, hunger, disease – involve rights denials;

☐ making choices between different types of development and different environmental strategies will, almost inevitably, involve a particular interpretation and prioritisation of rights;

☐ making wrong or risky choices about the environment will leave a sorry heritage for future generations – e.g. less productive land, less diversity of plant and animal life, less room for manoeuvre, fewer options – and thus involves rights questions of profound importance;

☐ global conflict continues to impede massively our ability to meet the development needs of the whole human community; it also has devastating environmental effects.

2. *The thinking of those at the broad focus of each field is increasingly marked by a shift away from a compartmentalised view of reality to an acceptance of the interconnectedness of all things and what has been called the 'permeability of boundaries'.*

For instance:

□ the local, national and global are viewed as different layers in a dynamic world system in which nothing finally makes sense save in relationship to everything else – the local, for instance, is in the global, the global in the local;

□ personal change and planetary change are, accordingly, held to be deeply interwoven processes;

□ past, present and future are conceived as being in dynamic relationship – real learning therefore involves looking to the future as well as at the present and past since our view of the future infuses how we see everything else.

'Ten things we could do to make the world a better place': Environmental and development issues in the middle school.

Cathie Holden

'If we all bought food from Traidcraft then the people who sell cape apples would go out of business and the peasants and workers would get paid for once.' This was one ten year old child's response to a class's effort to think of ways to make the world a better place. It arose after work involving learning about human rights, and thinking about the future.

The pupils initially drew up their own charter of the rights of children. These were then compared with the 'official' UN declaration and subsequently used in two ways: firstly as an enabling tool whereby children could remedy certain injustices in their school (no fountains, insanitary toilets), and secondly as a means of getting children to focus on those denied basic human rights. Inevitably this involved discussion of children in Ethiopia and South Africa (both in the news at the time). This brought the children round to discussing racism in this country and in this school, and led to a class charter being drawn up where racism wasn't allowed.[1]

This work was linked with work on the future. Time lines[2] were used to introduce children to the concept of looking towards the future, as were other techniques, such as planning towns and cities of the future. A key point in the learning process was the question: 'What ten things could we do to make the world a better place?' Some examples, as well as the one quoted earlier, were:

continued

2. try and be a ¾ vegetarian because if you are we don't kill as many animals and then they don't die out. Also if you had 3 fields and then fed them to a cow to make stake you could instead make loaves of bread and feed lots more people and you could give it to Ethiopians

We could use recycled paper. So that less trees are killed. If less trees <u>are</u> killed there would be more oxygen, and healthier people.

DON'T KILL ANIMALS FOR SKINS. wear other things. To help join GREEN PEACE. I am going to join

If every one put thier bottles in the bottle banks then the goverment would not spend so much on glass

Obviously the children's statements are rather simplistic – one cannot buy everything from Traidcraft, the government doesn't actually make bottles and giving loaves of bread to Ethiopians won't solve famine or inequalities between north and south. *But*, it does show the first glimmer of understanding of development and environmental issues, and it shows that pupils were aware that it is through working on these issues that a better future for all will be created. What is more, because of their previous work on human rights and on ways and means of working for these rights (for themselves and others) they were prepared to work towards carrying out these statements. A child brought in information on Greenpeace and others joined; money raised from a sponsored swim went to Oxfam and a local wildlife trust; information from Oxfam about their newspaper recycling scheme was photocopied and circulated; and one Wednesday the whole year base (90 children) set out for the bottle bank with carrier bags laden with bottles brought in by the entire school.

It isn't possible for ten year olds to stop global pollution, food mountains, famine or apartheid, but hopefully, by following the *think globally, act locally* slogan, children who have tried to protect their own environment, and who have thought about human rights, drawing up their own statements against racism and inequality, will become the responsible and politically aware adults of the future, able to work towards the protection of the planet, justice and peace.

References

1. For a fuller explanation see chapter by Starkey, H. and Holden, C., in *Global Teacher, Global Learner*, Pike, G. and Selby, D., Hodder & Stoughton, 1987.
2. This idea (and others on teaching about the world tomorrow) adapted from *World Studies 8-13*, Fisher, S. and Hicks, D., Oliver & Boyd, 1985.

Cathie Holden teaches at Bishop Kirk Middle School, Oxford.

Globbingo!

Globbingo! is a lively way of demonstrating the global in the local. Students are given a copy of the handout sheet (fig. 2) and are asked to fill in as many squares as possible by obtaining information from classmates. Having found someone who can answer one of the questions, the name of the country and the name of the person is written in the appropriate box. That person's name can appear only *once* on the sheet. Each time a row of boxes – horizontally, vertically or diagonally – is completed, students call out 'Globbingo!' Students will be surprised by the number of links they have with the wider world. After initial exploratory discussion, the class can be asked to categorise the types of global connection (e.g. trading links, media links, connections forged by the migration of peoples). A useful immediate follow-up exercise is to pin up a large world map and ask students to locate the countries identified by the activity. Colour-headed pins and cotton can be used to link each country with the locality. This creates a dramatic and colourful representation of the global in the local. Other follow-up ideas might be a 'world in the pantry' homework, in which students investigate the home pantry, cupboard or deep freeze and note the place of origin of each item, or a field trip to a local supermarket to explore the places of origin of the items on the shelves.

Figure 2

Find someone who:

A. has travelled to some foreign country
B. has a pen pal in another country
C. is learning a foreign language
D. has a relative in another country
E. has helped a visitor from another country
F. enjoys a music group from another country
G. is wearing something that was made in another country
H. enjoys eating foods from other countries
I. can name a famous sports star from another country

J. has a family car that was made in another country
K. has talked to someone who has lived in another country
L. lives in a home where more than one language is spoken
M. saw a story about another country in the newspaper recently
N. learned something about another country on TV recently
O. owns a TV or other appliance made in another country
P. has a parent or other relative who was born in another country

A	B	C	D
name	name	name	name
country	country	country	country
E	F	G	H
name	name	name	name
country	country	country	country
I	J	K	L
name	name	name	name
country	country	country	country
M	N	O	P
name	name	name	name
country	country	country	country

Some ideas for teaching and learning about the future

Newspapers Now
Students collect newspaper articles with the word 'future' in the title or articles with a strong futures orientation. These are pinned on a 'Futures' noticeboard or categorized in a scrapbook. In introducing the class to articles they bring to school, students can be asked to explain what is being said about the future and how it will effect classmates' lives.

Newspapers in the Future
Groups of students form writing/editorial teams to compile a *Future Times* (or other title of their choice). They agree on a date ten, twenty or thirty years into the future and cover local, national and global news through reports, editorials and illustrations. Advertisements can also be included! Each newspaper should contain a retrospective 'Life in (present year)' column.

Desirable Futures
Students, working individually, write a description of the world they would like to live in and of the lifestyle they desire for themselves in thirty years' time. They then form groups of 4–6 and, in turn, read their descriptions and face questions. The role of other members of the group is to play devil's advocate by asking questions concerning the achievability, realism, morality and implications for both the environment and other human beings of the future desired.

Posters
Students, working individually or in pairs, design posters reflecting their images of the future.

Visit
Students visit a city planning department or invite a city planner to visit the class to explain how the department sets about planning the local environment of the future.

Clock Face
Students, in groups, prepare a sixty-minute clock face on a large sheet of paper. Each minute represents fifty years. Different groups choose different areas of human activity, e.g. farming, transport and communications, medicine, industry. Using encyclopedias and reference books, they research major inventions and developments in their chosen area and write them in against the appropriate minute of the clock. The results will offer vivid evidence of the quickening pace of change. As a continuation, groups can prepare a second clock face on which one minute equals one year (the clock starts with the present). Keeping to the area of their choice, they discuss and predict likely future developments and when they will occur. These are written onto the clock face. Groups present their work and answer questions.

Attitudes to the Future
Students interview each other, friends, parents, relatives, teachers, etc., to find out their attitudes to, and hopes and fears for, the future. Alternatively, students design and use questionnaires.

continued

Model City
Students working in groups are asked to design a self-contained model city of approximately 50,000 people in which all the basic services (education, health care, water, power, waste disposal, recreation, transport, police, etc.) are provided. Groups are given four large sheets of white paper sellotaped together, rough paper and felt pens. They are also given different requirements and constraints under which to work, e.g. the city must be pollution free, it must only have public transport, it must occupy only one square mile of land area. After designing their city, groups present it to the rest of the class and answer questions.

What we take to be the present necessarily refers back and forward in time. Our reality grows out of past history, but is powerfully shaped too by what we believe about the future. Similarly, our decisions, the technologies we collectively employ, the ideologies and ends we pursue all frame and condition the world of our descendants. In other words, whatever we do we cannot be uninvolved. This is immensely important for such a view leads to a deep sense of historical process and connectedness in space and time.

Richard Slaughter[28]

A common acknowledgement of the 'permeability of boundaries' also explains why those at the broad focus:

☐ emphasise the importance of interdisciplinary approaches and call for the infusion of the whole school curriculum with a global perspective;

☐ seek a more thoroughgoing integration of school and community through greater involvement of the community in school life and through an expansion of in-community learning opportunities;

☐ regard education as a lifelong process infusing every aspect of human activity rather than as a part of life that ends with leaving school, college or university.

3. *The broad focus position within each of the four 'educations' involves fostering the attitudes and prac- tising the skills necessary for active participation in the political process. Such attitudes and skills are empowering and vital if students are to become subjects rather than objects in their own history.*

This is why such great emphasis is laid upon participatory learning and upon creating a humane, open and democratic classroom marked by high levels of self and group esteem, co-operation, debate, discussion and negotiation (see pages 51–57).

A thought-provoking way to think about the four 'educations' is to see their relationship as *holographic*. A hologram is a three-dimensional 'photograph' created by laser technology. Amongst its most astonishing properties is that *the part contains the code of the whole*. Hence, a hologram of a face, if broken, can be reconstructed from, say, the hologram of the nose. Similarly, a maturer and more comprehensive understanding of, for instance, environmental education will, whatever the nature of one's initial interest, inevitably lead to questions of development, rights, culture, race, gender and peaceful and conflictual relationships. *The field carries the code of the whole; it can be conceived of as both part of the whole and the whole.*

... 'I'm sure I don't know,' the Lion growled out as he lay down again. 'There was too much dust to see anything. What a time the Monster is cutting up that cake!'
Alice had seated herself on the bank of a little brook, with the great dish on her knees, and was sawing away diligently with the knife. 'It's very provoking!' she said, in reply to the Lion (she was getting quite used to being called 'the Monster'). 'I've cut several slices already, but they always join on again!' 'You don't know how to manage looking-glass cakes,' the Unicorn remarked. 'Hand it round first, and cut it afterwards.'
This sounded nonsense, but Alice very obediently got up, and carried the dish round, and the cake divided itself into three pieces as she did so. 'Now cut it up,' said the Lion, as she returned to her place with the empty dish ...
Lewis Carroll, *Through the Looking Glass*

For that reason, some think that little is lost, and, perhaps, much gained by having different fields working towards the same end. For that reason, too, some proponents of each field argue that *theirs* is *the* field. Others warn of the dangers of fragmentation, and curriculum overload and of the likelihood of duplication when funding is in short supply.

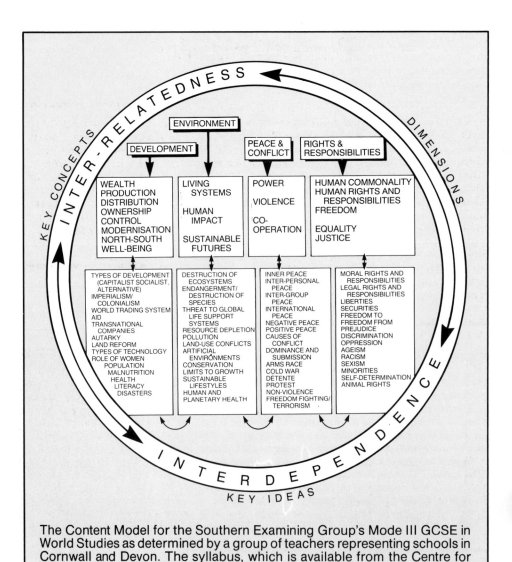

The Content Model for the Southern Examining Group's Mode III GCSE in World Studies as determined by a group of teachers representing schools in Cornwall and Devon. The syllabus, which is available from the Centre for Global Education, suggests an holistic model for understanding the world.

Person/planet

The diagram on this page (fig. 3) provides a holistic model for education. It suggests an interplay between three 'outer' realities – our 'close reality' (personal and local), our 'intermediate reality' (regional and national) and our 'distant reality' (the wider world). The three are interwoven; each dependent on the others for its particular form and direction. Schools need to reflect the dynamic relationship between different spatial levels. The diagram also suggests a constant interplay between past, present and future. Our present is shaped by our past but is also informed by our hopes and expectations for the future. Schools also need to offer opportunities for students to study, reflect upon and discuss possible, probable and preferred futures. The shaded area on the diagram represents the predominant focus of attention in schools – the 'close and immediate reality' in the past and present with a nodding, usually careers-oriented, reference to the immediate future.

In the heaven of Indra, there is said to be a network of pearls, so arranged that if you look at one you see all the others reflected in it. In the same way each object in the world is not merely itself but involves every other object, and in fact is every other object.

The Flower Garland Sutra

Figure 3

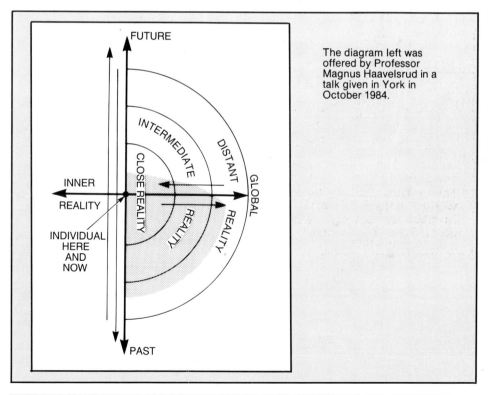

The diagram left was offered by Professor Magnus Haavelsrud in a talk given in York in October 1984.

Left unshaded is our 'inner' reality which, the diagram suggests, is in constant interplay with our multi-layered 'outer reality'. What we are affects our picture of the world and what the world is affects our picture of ourselves. An emerging awareness of the world goes hand in glove with a growing self-awareness. As many people who have made voyages of discovery have found, they learn as much about themselves as about the new landscape they enter. *The outward journey is also the inward journey. The two journeys are complementary and mutually illuminating.*

A student brought face to face with new perspectives, new ways of seeing the world, alternative visions of the future; a student learning that her life is inextricably bound up with the problems and prospects of peoples and environments thousands of miles away, will inevitably begin to critically examine her assumptions, perspectives, values and behaviour. *The journey outward is the journey inward.* Likewise, carefully and sensitively coaxed, *the journey inwards is the journey outwards.* As Theodore Roszak describes it: 'suddenly, as we grow more introspectively inquisitive about the deep powers of the personality, our ethical concern becomes more universal than ever before; it strives to embrace the natural beauties and all sentient beings, each in her and his and its native peculiarity. Introspection and universality: centre and circumference. Personal awareness burrows deeper into itself; our sense of belonging reaches out further. It all happens at once, the concentration of mind, the expansion of loyalty.'[29]

> *The man who sat on the ground in his tipi meditating on life and its meaning, accepting the kinship of all creatures and acknowledging unity with the universe of things was infusing into his being the true essence of civilization. And when native man left off this form of development, his humanization was retarded in growth.*
>
> Chief Luther Standing Bear

Relearn the alphabet,
relearn the world, the world
understood anew only in doing, understood only as
looked-up-into out of earth,
the heart an eye looking,
the heart a root
planted in earth.
Transmutation is not
under the will's rule.

Denise Levertov

The person/planet relationship has enormous implications for schools. Once understood, we see that it is not finally possible to promote planetary consciousness in the classroom without the corresponding promotion of self-discovery.

Interestingly and significantly, those at the leading edge of the fields reviewed earlier have begun to foster the 'journey inward'. Steve van Matre's acclimatization programmes[30] have emphasised that true environmental understanding must be informed by feelings, emotions and personal involvement and that students can learn to see themselves in new ways through contact with the natural world. Sandy Parker, a peace educator, emphasises the importance of exploring our 'inner ecology' (see this page) whilst other peace educators have developed activities for finding 'inner peacefulness'. ('We all have the Cold War within us'.) Those at the leading edge have each in their own way arrived at the conviction that the well-being of the planet is inextricably bound up with the achievement of full and authentic personhood.

We shall not cease from exploration
And the end of all our exploring
Will be to arrive where we started
And know the place for the first time.
T.S. Eliot, *Little Gidding*

Earth Education

Jon Cree

Earth Education is a widely known approach to environmental education that has been developed by the Institute for Earth Education, whose overall goal is 'the process of helping people of all ages live more harmoniously and joyously with the natural world'. A goal fundamental to both development and environmental education.

To achieve this goal, there is an urgent need to develop *complete* educational programmes that break down barriers to the natural world, encourage an understanding of how ecosystems work, and develop positive caring attitudes to the earth ... a few isolated environmental activities are not enough. Therefore the Institute for Earth Education designed a range of structured programmes which incorporate these aims.

Earth Caretakers is one such programme which starts in the classroom with the arrival of a slightly battered box. Upon opening the box a dustbin is revealed. With the help of Rangers Roger and Rachel the class analyse the waste in the dustbin and look at the resources and energy involved in its making. They then investigate the effects of our (human) careless use of energy and resources on endangered species. Letters from the Rangers invite the class to train as earth caretakers so that they can help the earth and its non-human inhabitants. The first stage of this training helps the children learn five secrets of the earth and answer a riddle posed by the Rangers. The class spend a day in a natural setting reawakening their senses on an earthwalk, participating in a series of activities on a concept path that helps them understand energy flow, looking for the lost letters to help them discover the natural world, and spending some time alone developing easy, quiet relationships with the natural world. Back in the classroom further

continued

Right: Humming bird and nectar plant.
Above: On the street surveying a 'rubbish collecting worm'.

letters from the Rangers help the class explore the fifth secret, that of care, and they work on their environmental bad habits such as wasting energy in the classroom. Once the class has found the five secrets and answered the riddle, another riddle is posed by the Rangers. This leads on to three further ecological concepts: the cycling of the natural materials of life; interrelationships between all living things and how everything on the earth is in a process of changing.

This complete programme incorporates an adventuresome, magical learning experience that focuses on specific outcomes. If the future of the planet is to be secured, it is essential that more programmes such as these are designed and practised.

Jon Cree is a Day Visits Organiser at Losehill Hall, Peak National Park Centre, Castleton, Derbyshire.

For further information about Earth Education, and details of programmes offered in other areas of the U.K. contact: Stewart Anthony, 6 Wicklands Road, Hunsdon, Nr Ware, Herts.

'My argument,' writes Roszak, 'is that *the needs of the planet are the needs of the person.* And, therefore, *the rights of the person are the rights of the planet* ... the adventure of self-discovery stands before us as the most practical of pleasures.'[31]

Inner Ecology

Sandy Parker

We can see ourselves as being at the centre of a triangle of interdependent relationships:

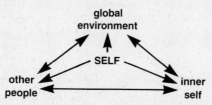

The way we view the world is often a reflection of the way we view ourselves:
   If I am despairing of myself, I despair of the world's future;
   If I am hopeful for myself, I have hope for the world;
   If I am uncaring of myself, I am careless of my environment and of my sister creatures;
   If I am loving, I see the world as cooperative and caring;
   If I feel helpless, I see the world at the mercy of events;
   If I feel empowered, I see myself making a difference to my friends and my environment;
The outer world acts as a mirror to my inner world.

If 'ecology' is concerned with 'the relationships of living organisms to their surroundings, their habits and their modes of life' (O.E.D.) then perhaps we can call a concern for our inner world 'inner ecology'. And our inner ecology will be an important dimension of our attitudes to environmental and development issues.

Talking with teenagers in schools, I notice how often they wish to avoid thinking about the future:
   It's too frightening to think about;
   There's no point in thinking about the future, you can't do anything about it, and anyway there probably won't be one!
Unsurprising with a disaster oriented media. Can I help and encourage students to develop a more positive inner ecology – to become aware of the enabling power of their own thoughts, imagination and hopes?

I describe one classroom exercise that I have used with various age groups – the setting: a quiet room; some quietly relaxing music available; large sheets of drawing paper; sets of pastel crayons. After an initial short relaxation I invite the students to join me on a journey in their imagination. We explore some favourite and familiar places. We slowly leave planet earth,

continued

journeying into space, sharing the vision of the astronauts. Returning we find all subtly changed. Earth has become the planet of our hopes and dreams. We explore and notice the changes. Time is allowed for drawing or writing something about the earth of our hopes and dreams.

Next we move on, returning briefly to our visualization, to discover how we fit into that planet: what our place in it is. Again we express this by drawing or writing. Finally we each take time to think what quality of character we need to enable us to help this come about: love; courage; patience; anger; strength; impatience; determination (all recently chosen by a group of 15 years olds).

Such an exercise must, of course, be firmly grounded with accurate factual knowledge and study, but equally must *not* be limited by my adult assumptions about what is 'possible'. Students may find the exercise difficult, and most seem to find it empowering. A colleague who observed one group wrote:

> your lessons made them think beyond the bounds of their own needs and experiences ... Initial feelings about the future were pessimistic, but most of the students felt more optimistic about the future and the part they could play in it because of your lessons.

One student in another group produced this drawing after a similar exercise:

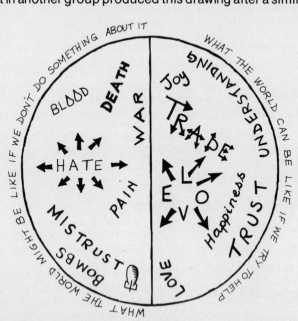

Sandy Parker, formerly Head of Religious Education at Ackworth School, Pontefract, is now a Research Fellow at the Centre for Global Education, University of York.

Some aims for education

*'Cheshire-Puss,' she began, rather timidly ...' would you tell
me, please, which way I ought to go from here?'*
*'That depends a good deal on where you want to get to,' said
the cat.*
'I don't much care where ...' said Alice.
'Then it doesn't matter which way you go,' said the cat.
Lewis Carroll, *Alice in Wonderland*

What, then, might be the aims of an education which takes
into account the needs of both person and planet? It is clear
that an appropriate education will have an holistic approach
to learning; education will be regarded as a lifelong process
in which schooling plays an important part. The school will
work in partnership with the home and the community,
providing educational experiences for young people. Within
school itself, attention will be paid to the whole school
experience of a student, not just her academic achievement;
similarly, aims such as those outlined below will be regarded
as applicable right across the curriculum, not only in the
humanities or social studies areas.

1 Systems

*Students should understand the systemic nature of the
world*

Firstly, in a spatial dimension: changes in any one part, at
whatever level (personal to global), can affect the whole.
Processes and factors that bring about change operate
within an interrelated and interdependent system.

Secondly, in a temporal dimension: interpretations of the
present grow out of past history but are profoundly shaped
too by beliefs about the future.

Thirdly, in an issues dimension: contemporary global
problems can only be finally understood as malfunctions of
a system, not as unconnected issues. Effective solutions are
helpful adjustments within the system.

Students should understand the principles of ecology

The components of an ecosystem are in dynamic equilibrium with adjustments continually taking place. The vital

stability of ecosystems can be threatened through the short-sighted actions of humankind.

Students should understand the relationship of person to planet

---

For the potential of the oak lies vibrating within the atomic structure of the acorn, as does the flower live within the bud and the Self within man.
Master Subramuniya,
Cognizantability

An individual is an integral part of the global system. Humankind lives in complex interrelationship with environmental systems: the well-being of person and planet are interdependent. A personal exploration of the wider world can lead to greater self-awareness, just as heightened self-awareness can aid and enlarge understanding of global issues.

Students should recognise the extent of their potential

Human potential can only be fully realised when the physical, emotional, intellectual and spiritual dimensions of personhood are seen as indivisible and complementary. Students should be encouraged, through heightening their levels of self-awareness and self-esteem, to awaken their full potential and, hence, achieve higher levels of personal autonomy and empowerment.

2 Perspectives

Students should recognise that their worldview is not universally shared

Everyone interprets the world from within a particular framework of perception and thought. Personal perspectives are shaped by such factors as age, class, creed, culture, ethnicity, gender, geographical context, ideology, language, nationality and race. There are difficulties and dangers inherent in using one's own perspective as a yardstick by which to judge the values and behaviour of others.

Students should be receptive to other perspectives

An ability to empathise with other people, to see the world through their eyes can be profoundly liberating. It can help to challenge unexamined assumptions, feed imagination and promote creative thought and action: it can lead to a radical reassessment of both problems and solutions.

When I first drove along the Stuart Highway north of Taylor Crossing to Warabri I heartily agreed with those who had said it was the most barren stretch of country they had ever encountered. I couldn't cover the distance fast enough. Now I can drive barely a mile without seeing something worthy of

---

comment. In what was once spinifex plains broken only by the odd acacia stand, I now see high differentiated foraging grounds, rich in small fruits and goanna; in burnt-out plains, I now see prime hunting-ground and I wonder 'whose fire burnt here?' Local people always know who has lit a fire because only persons in correct relationship to a particular tract of land may do so. In the wide dry creek beds, I now find the wild potato runners; I recognize the potential water sources, the places where frogs may be hidden deep in the cool damp sand. I scan the horizon for smoke; I see a red tinge in the rock and I look for the ochre.

Diane Bell, *Daughters of the Dreaming*

Students should appreciate what other cultures have to offer

An awareness and appreciation of diverse cultural view-points and experiences can be life-enriching and can deepen understanding of the global system. Complementary to this is an appreciation of what humankind holds in common.

3 Conditions

Students should understand global conditions, trends and developments

Knowledge about major global conditions is necessary for understanding the global system. These would include: sources and distribution of power and wealth; processes and types of development; the impact of human activity, including science and technology, on the environment; the dynamics of conflict and co-operation; setbacks and success stories in the safeguarding of human rights. Informed understanding develops from familiarity with a range of arguments – often conflicting – surrounding those conditions, trends and developments and a capacity to reflect upon the long-term consequences of a range of options.

Students should have a concern for justice, rights and responsibilities

Global conditions give rise to, and nurture, many examples of unjust relationships and dependencies. A concern for justice entails achieving a delicate balance between asserting one's rights and recognising one's responsibilities towards safeguarding the rights of others and of the planet.

4 Actions

Students should recognise the implications of present choices and actions

Choices made and actions taken have repercussions throughout the global system. Present choices and actions, both individual and collective, can have implications for the future well-being of humankind and the environment. Failure to choose and act carries implications that can be as significant as conscious choice and action.

Students should develop the action skills necessary for constructive participation in global society.

Decision-making, choice and judgement – important components of constructive participation at all levels of democratic society – require the practice and refinement of social and political skills.

Schools in a world of change

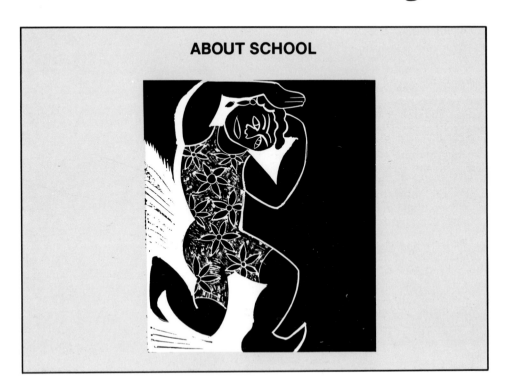

ABOUT SCHOOL

He always wanted to say things. But no one understood.
He always wanted to explain things. But no one cared.
So he drew.

Sometimes he would just draw and it wasn't anything.
He wanted to carve it in stone or write it in the sky.
He would lie out on the grass and look up in the sky
and it would be only him and the sky and the things
inside that needed saying.

And it was after that, that he drew the picture.
It was a beautiful picture. He kept it under the
pillow and would let no one see it.
And he would look at it every night and think about it.
And when it was dark, and his eyes were closed, he
could still see it.
And it was all of him. And he loved it.

When he started school he brought it with him.
Not to show anyone, but just to have it with him like a
friend.

It was funny about school.
He sat in a square, brown desk like all the other
square, brown desks and he thought it should be red.
And his room was a square, brown room. Like all the
other rooms.
And it was tight and close. And stiff.

He hated to hold the pencil and the chalk, with his arm
stiff and his feet flat on the floor, with the teacher
watching and watching.
And then he had to write numbers. And they weren't
anything.
They were worse than the letters that could be
something if you put them together.
And the numbers were tight and square and he hated the
whole thing.

The teacher came and spoke to him. She told him to
wear a tie like all the other boys. He said he didn't
like them and she said it didn't matter.

After that they drew. And he drew all yellow and it
was the way he felt about morning. And it was
beautiful.

continued

The teacher came and smiled at him 'What's this?' she said. 'Why don't you draw something like Ken's drawing? Isn't that beautiful?'
It was all questions.

After that his mother bought him a tie and he always drew airplanes and rocket ships like everyone else.
And he threw the old picture away.
And when he lay out alone looking at the sky, it was big and blue and all of everything, but he wasn't anymore.

He was square inside and brown, and his hands were stiff, and he was like anyone else. And the thing inside him that needed saying didn't need saying anymore.

It had stopped pushing. It was crushed. Stiff. Like everything else.

It is easy to criticise schools. Underfunded, under-resourced, bombarded from all sides by new policy requirements, new examination demands, the vicarious whims of local and national government, the constraints of union practice, the concerns of parents and employers ... schools have become battlegrounds where daily the values and practices of an older, established order try to fend off the relentless and unco-ordinated attacks spawned by the disorder and challenges of the late twentieth century. In the midst of the battlefield young people grapple to come to terms with a world of which the most salient feature, perhaps, is the speed at which it moves on. For the school student of today new challenges pile up upon the part-digested forms of earlier concerns. Not just the pursuit of qualifications, but also the prospect of unemployment; not just the anxieties of sexual freedom, but also the traumas of Aids; not only the dangers of nuclear weapons, but also the perils to the earth's life support systems from pollution, deforestation and urbanisation. All of these new challenges, of course, have repercussions throughout the global system and implications for the future of the planet which may well go far beyond our present understanding.

How can schools cope? The aims outlined above suggest that some radical reforms of common perceptions and patterns of schooling are needed. Piecemeal responses to the latest challenge – a new curriculum focus, a specially-created post of responsibility, a fresh policy statement – may have limited effect if they fail to grasp the totality of the situation and, hence, are quickly superceded by the next demand. Reforms to curriculum content – the most common response in schools to the new challenges of the global system – are, by themselves, insufficient to meet the needs of future global citizens. The microchip revolution, for example, has created a demand for the knowledge and skills of computer literacy; it has also generated the need for awareness of, and ability to cope with, the radical transformation that this technology is already bringing to areas such as employment, family life and personal freedoms. A substantial rethinking of the *process* of schooling is required if the students of today are to sustain and nurture a world for which, as Jean Houston noted earlier (see page 3), those presently responsible are ill-equipped.

The process of schooling
Teaching and learning methods

Marshall McLuhan's observation, 'the medium is the message', provides some valuable insights when applied to the process of learning in the classroom. If the 'medium' of learning is characterised by individual competition, working in silence, a compartmentalisation of knowledge into subject areas, an emphasis on learning through abstract concepts rather than by direct experience and a devaluing of personal feelings, what are the 'messages' the students receive? Are these messages appropriate to education for life in an interdependent, fast-changing world? The aims outlined above imply that a rather different learning process is required, if medium and message are to be in harmony.

Woolly Thinking

Resources For a class of thirty students: 10 sheets of sugar paper, 10 sets of labels (3 per set and each set of a different colour), 30 pins, scrap paper and 10 balls of wool of colours to match the labels. A large open space in the classroom is required so that the following arrangement is possible:

continued

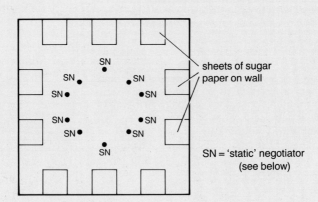

sheets of sugar paper on wall

SN = 'static' negotiator (see below)

Ten selected topics are written up at the top of the sugar paper, one on each sheet. Topics could be: The Arms Race, Environmental Pollution, Unemployment, Third World Underdevelopment, Terrorism/Freedom Fighting, Human Rights Violations, Nationalism, Natural Resource Depletion, Malnutrition, Urbanisation. The topics should also be written on the sets of labels.

Procedure. Students choose one of the ten topics by standing next to a particular sheet of sugar paper. There should be no more than three students per group. Each student should wear a label identifying them as representing that particular topic. Groups first brainstorm relevant factors (i.e. causes/effects) surrounding their topic using the scrap paper provided. They then appoint a 'static' negotiator and two 'mobile' negotiators. The 'static' negotiators should take up positions in a circle and tie the ends of their balls of wool around their waists. Their role is to stay in one position but to join in negotiations with any of the 'mobile' negotiators of the nine other groups. The role of the 'mobile' negotiator is to go out and negotiate; the purpose of negotiation is to try to establish links, connections or relationships between any two topics.

Each time a connection has been discussed and agreed, two balls of wool are passed across the circle and looped around the waists of the 'static' negotiators of the two groups concerned. It is important that the wool is kept taut and that the ball is brought back to the 'static' negotiator from whom it started each time. It is also very important that the thinking behind each agreement is recorded by 'mobile' negotiators of both groups on their respective sheets of sugar paper. As the activity continues, a spider's web of connections between the ten issues will be produced; the web will probably be so closely woven that 'mobile' negotiators will have to crawl underneath in pursuit of their task.

The web of different coloured wools offers a potent visual symbol of the interlocking/systemic nature of contemporary global issues. Throughout discussion following the activity it is helpful to keep the web intact. This can be done by asking 'static' negotiators to sit down where they have been standing.

Class members can be encouraged to describe the negotiations in which they were involved and to reflect upon the connections made during the activity. Discussion of the absence of connections can also be very productive.

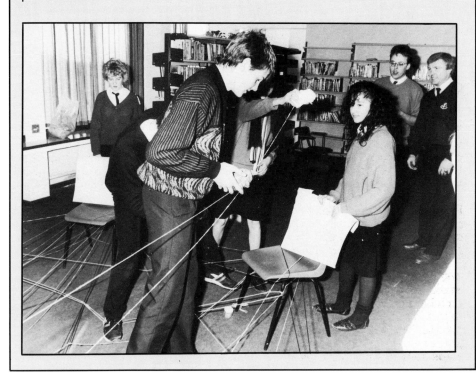

An example of a more appropriate medium can be found in the activity *Woolly Thinking*. Through participating in this activity students discover for themselves the interdependent nature of major global issues as they create an intricate woollen web of connections. The 'hands-on' experience of the web construction, and the stunning multi-coloured symbol created, appeal to those learners who perceive information more readily when it is presented in concrete as well as abstract forms. The process of negotiation between participants helps to develop important skills of communication, analysis and judgement and encourages creative thinking. *Woolly Thinking* can contribute, too, to students' understanding of global conditions, trends and developments; either as an initial activity to stimulate thinking and subsequent research on global issues, or as a culmination of work already undertaken. As with many such interactive exercises for the classroom the 'content' – the topics – can be varied to suit the needs and abilities of different age groups. Primary and lower secondary teachers have successfully used *Woolly Thinking* to aid students' understanding of the food web and other types of ecological interdependence; local community interdependencies, between residents and tradespeople, have also been vividly illustrated in this way.

Such activities enable the broad aims to be met in ways which are themselves consistent with those aims. The general thrust of this learning process embodies a shift away from a dependence upon cognitive learning alone towards more holistic approaches in which the complementary capacities of reason and emotion, intellect and imagination, analysis and intuition are harmonised.

> *After you understand all about the sun and the stars and rotation of the earth, you may still miss the radiance of the sunset.*
> Alfred North Whitehead

The ability to empathise with another person, for example, may require a student to take an imaginative leap outside her own cultural framework and, in Harper Lee's words, 'to climb into his skin and walk around in it'. Such mental agility is unlikely to result from intellectual reasoning alone, but rather from a constant interplay between knowledge, imagination and intuition. The emotional 'slap on the face' which so often accompanies a sudden realisation of the limitations to one's world view is a powerful tool for learning, a deep-felt dawning which can stimulate the intellect into accommodating new horizons glimpsed.

In practice, the classroom which adopts an holistic learning approach will feature structured pair and small group activity, thereby encouraging communication, co-operation, negotiation and decision-making skills; role play, simulation games and experiential activities (short activities designed to stimulate learning through involving participants in an intense direct experience), enabling students to explore their own attitudes and perspectives and to consider other viewpoints and feelings; and the controlled use of guided fantasy and visualisation to activate creative thinking and problem solving processes. Individual study, teacher input and constructive competition are not eschewed altogether but regarded as components which, together with other approaches mentioned, make up the ecological balance of the classroom.

It would be wrong to imagine that holistic learning may be employed at the expense of high levels of cognitive attainment; that these approaches, in other words, are no

SALLY FORTH   by Greg Howard

good for promoting literacy or passing examinations. There is a substantial body of research evidence which shows that participatory learning, an affirmative classroom environment and the development of open, trusting and empathetic relationships among teachers and students all lead to higher levels of cognitive attainment, for both able and less able students, than in classrooms where the emphasis is on individualistic work and competitive personal relationships[32]. Furthermore, co-operative learning has been found to be more efficient than individual or competitive study the higher the level of conceptual understanding required by a particular task[33]. There would seem to be significant implications arising from this research for teaching and learning methods most apposite to a consideration of complex global issues.

Classroom climate

Democracy is best learned in a democratic setting where participation is encouraged, where views can be expressed openly and discussed, where there is freedom of expression for pupils and teachers, and where there is fairness and justice. An appropriate climate is, therefore, an essential complement to effective learning about human rights.

Recommendation of the Committee of Ministers to Member States on Teaching and Learning about Human Rights in Schools. Council of Europe, 1985

Crucial to the process of holistic learning is the climate of the classroom – the character and quality of interpersonal relations between teacher and students and among students themselves. Such learning is unlikely to take place unless an affirmative environment prevails, in which the integral worth and experience of each individual is cherished and, consequently, their self-concept enhanced. An affirmative classroom is built upon a horizontal

One day Mulla Nasrudin found a tortoise. He tied it to his belt and continued his work in the fields. The tortoise started to struggle. The Mulla held it up and asked: 'What's the matter, don't you want to learn how to plough?'
Idries Shah,
The Subtleties of the Inimitable Mulla Nasrudin

pattern of relationships, involving peer learning and the active participation of students in the initiation, direction and evaluation of what is learnt, rather than the vertical or top-downward pattern in which the teacher acts as fountainhead of knowledge.

Diamond Ranking

Resources Nine brief statements or photographs representing a spread of opinion, perspectives or images for each pair of students. Each statement/ photograph should be given a short title or number for easy reference. Each set of nine should be cut up and stored in an envelope.

Procedure Pairs are given an envelope containing the nine statements/ photographs and are asked to rank them in diamond formation, i.e.

A fairly loose criterion for ranking is given such as 'importance', 'significance', 'interest', the teacher resisting any requests for her to be more specific about the criterion. The most 'important', 'significant' or 'interesting' statement/photograph is placed at the top of the diamond. The next two are placed in second equal position. The three across the centre are fourth equal. The next two are seventh equal. The statement/photograph placed at the foot of the diamond is the one considered by the pair to be the least 'important', 'significant' or 'interesting'. When pairs have completed their task, they form into sixes. Each pair explains and seeks to justify its ranking to the other two pairs. The six then try to negotiate a consensus ranking for the group as a whole. Plenary reporting back and discussion follows. The imprecise criterion given is itself likely to be one layer in the discussion. What does 'importance', 'significance' or 'interesting' mean? Should we try and pin down what we mean more precisely? Skills used in this activity include prioritisation, discussion, negotiation, accommodation to other perspectives, and consensus-seeking. In the plenary, a group reporting their inability to agree upon a ranking order is as important a discussion point as a group reporting that they have achieved consensus.

Diamond ranking provides an example of horizontal learning in practice. This activity helps students in an unthreatening way to clarify their thoughts and feelings about a particular subject whilst alerting them to a range of other opinions and perspectives. Underpinning the activity is the unspoken assumption that every participant has something relevant and valuable to bring to the discussion. The progression towards consensus, first in pairs then in groups of six, encourages constructive dialogue rather than a polarisation of viewpoints. As with many such interactive group discussion activities, the realisation that there is not a single or simple 'right answer' conveys important messages to students concerning the quest for solutions to global problems. The nine photographs or statements – and the attendant criterion for ranking – can, of course, be varied to suit age and ability levels; they can also be used to stimulate in-depth study of the themes or issues they convey.

And what of the teacher's role in the affirmative, participatory classroom? 'We are,' says Carl Rogers, 'faced with an entirely new situation in education where the goal of education, if we are to survive, is the *facilitation of change and learning*'[34]. In the affirmative classroom the teacher acts as facilitator of students' learning, using her skills and experience to draw out and advise upon a natural process of change and personal growth.

Effective facilitation not only requires sensitivity and skill, it also necessitates a devolution of power within the classroom. The teacher uses her expertise and status not to compel or instruct but to empower her students on their journeys towards personal autonomy and the fulfilment of their potential. This shift in the locus of power and decision-making in the classroom is an important safeguard against the risk of indoctrination on the part of the teacher; participatory learning ensures that a range of perspectives and opinions are aired and the skills of discernment and judgement honed.

> *You cannot teach a man anything.*
> *You can only help him discover it within himself.*
>
> Galileo

Education for action

If the generation now at school is to be any better equipped to bear the enormous responsibility for the planetary process to which Jean Houston referred, students urgently need to practise and refine action-oriented skills. The development of capacities required to deal constructively with personal and global change, to work for justice and the defence of human rights, to contribute towards the realisation of a preferred future for the planet can no longer be left to chance or be considered inappropriate for schooling. 'We must', argue David Shirman and David

> *Three things cannot be retrieved:*
> *the arrow once sped from the bow;*
> *the word spoken in haste;*
> *the missed opportunity.*
>
> Ali the Lion, Caliph of Islam, son-in-law of Mohammed the Prophet

Conrad, 'encourage and assist our students in identifying their own value and action priorities in light of their concern about particular global issues. We must help them discover their own strengths and learn how they can be most effective. We must help each person find his or her entry point for action.'[35] This goal is unlikely to be achieved unless schools provide opportunities – and support – for students to become involved in social and political processes both within and beyond the school grounds. Education for democracy will be most effective in a democratic school, where medium and message are in harmony; education for a fast-changing, interdependent world will be best served by helping students to develop and practise action skills which will enable them·to become agents, rather than servants of change.

'Entry points for action' in the school might include:

☐ participation in the management of the school through full representation on decision-making committees;

☐ establishing discussion and action groups to consider responses to local, national and international concerns;

☐ promoting planet-conscious campaigns such as recycling paper waste, reducing energy consumption or challenging the needless exploitation of animals;

☐ establishing a school garden to produce organically grown food for consumption at school;

☐ promoting letter-writing campaigns on behalf of individuals or groups in the local, national or international community;

☐ establishing links with schools in very different communities to promote the exchange of experiences, views and perspectives.

Outside school entry points (following in-school discussion and planning) might include:

☐ campaigning for, or establishing, kindergartens, playgrounds, parks and play-groups where needed;

☐ participation in the work of a local, national or international environmental or development organisation;

☐ running a planet-conscious home by, for example, conserving energy, recycling waste products, repairing broken goods whenever possible;

☐ assessing facilities for the disabled in the local community and campaigning on their behalf for improvements;

☐ questioning candidates for local and national elections on their views on major global issues;

☐ writing, producing and distributing a newspaper for young people providing information on relevant local and global issues and suggestions for those who want to become involved.

The French movement of cooperative schools and cooperative classes provides many good examples of action skills in practice. A school or a class can become a cooperative with the aim of promoting educational, cultural or social activities. Any funds, raised from a variety of sources, which are required for the project are administered on behalf of the group as a cooperative and including students on the committee. The projects can be part of the school curriculum or an extra-curricular activity. Examples include class journeys; ecological projects such as reclamation schemes; attempts to restore life and dignity to run-down neighbourhoods by initiating discussions with other local organisations; a school radio station; school to school exchanges and correspondence. The essence is the formal involvement of the students and a desire to involve the local community and parents in the project.
Hugh Starkey[36]

Beginning early

Infant and junior school children are often considered too young to learn about the serious difficulties besetting our planet. Such topics, it is held, should be reserved for the secondary school. Now a growing body of research and writing suggests that schools should begin to implement and systematically develop a global perspective from the very beginning of the primary school years.

The infant classroom needs to lay the foundations of a planet-conscious education programme by strengthening each child's sense of her own worth and by developing communication and co-operation skills. Children with a high self-regard, research suggests, are likely to be more altruistic, generous and sharing in nature[37]. They will also exhibit more positive attitudes to others, including those in distress, if they have learnt to express their thoughts and feelings clearly and have learnt to listen carefully[38]. Co-operative learning contexts will build supporting and caring attitudes and reinforce self-image through the elimination of failure. 'By directly participating in [co-operative] activities, children can, at a very early age, gain concrete experience of the highly complex concept of interdependence. This notion will be essential to later studies of relationships between ethnic groups and countries, of ecosystems, of world economics, and of public health, to name but a few areas of applicability.'[39] Esteem-building, communication and cooperative games, and learning experiences for the infant classroom are now abundantly available, their flavour and purpose being neatly caught in the title of one of the many excellent teacher handbooks – *The Friendly Classroom for a Small Planet*[40].

Towards a Global Perspective in the Early Childhood Years

Susan Fountain

Relationships between living organisms are essentially cooperative; to understand ecosystems, global economics, or interactions between nations, a grasp of the concept of interdependence is vital. Is 'interdependence' too sophisticated an idea for an early childhood curriculum? My experience as a teacher of young children at the International School of Geneva suggests that practical cooperative experiences can lay the foundation for later global awareness.

For example, in the game 'Frozen Bean Bag'[1], children move around the room balancing bean bags on their heads. If a bean bag falls off that child is 'frozen' in place until someone replaces the bean bag. They realize quickly that they must rely on each other for help, and have a tremendous amount of fun while cooperating! A 'Class Web' can be made by having children stand in a circle and pass a ball of wool from one to the other. Once all are joined together in the web, they can try rotating or moving about the room, keeping the web intact. The experience, at once symbolic and concrete, shows that individual actions are not isolated, but affect the group as a whole. Such activities, however, are most effective when embedded in a cooperatively-oriented program: one in which competition in learning is de-emphasized in favour of activities which require input from all in order to reach a goal; in which children have an active part in classroom decision-making; in which conflicts are treated as opportunities to learn the process of generating alternative solutions, not simply 'solved' by an authority figure.

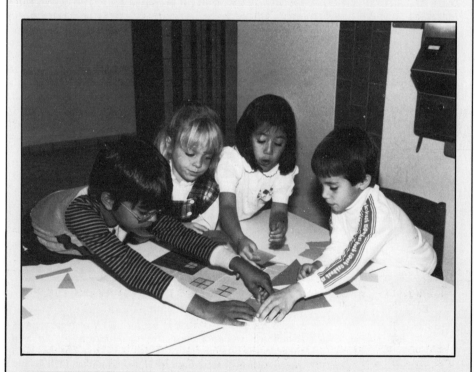

Strong communication skills facilitate cooperation and understanding of other points of view. Abundant opportunities for child–child and child–teacher communication should occur throughout the day. Specific activities might include cooperative storytelling, each child in turn contri-

continued

buting a line that follows logically. This requires good listening, and the ability to clearly convey one's ideas. So does the favourite game 'Police Officer, Have You Seen My Friend?'[2]. One child describes a member of the group in terms of her/his positive attributes ('she's good at painting', 'he helps people on the playground', etc.) to a child acting as the police officer, who must then guess who that person is. It is a highly affirming experience to be thus described!

And affirming experiences support children in communicating and cooperating effectively. Strong self-esteem has been shown to correlate with many measures of prosocial adjustment[3]. Having each child make an 'Affirmation Notebook'[4] is one of my favourite self-concept building techniques. Pages can include self-portraits, writing (or dictating) about favourite activities, what makes the child feel happy (or angry, sad, frightened), what the child likes about her/himself, and comments from other children on what they like about that person, to name but a few possibilities. However, the development of a strong self-concept obviously goes on outside of such structured activities as well; affirmation should be a part of daily classroom interactions.

The early childhood years are an exceptionally receptive time of life. Preconceptions about self-image, the importance of competition, conflict resolution styles, etc., may not yet be rigidly set. The opportunity to make a positive impact on this age group through work on affirmation, communication, and co-operation should not be missed!

References:

1. Orlick, T., *The Cooperative Sports and Games Book*, Writers and Readers Publishing Cooperative, London, 1978.

2. Borba, M. and Borba, C., *Self-Esteem: A Classroom Affair*, Winston Press, Minneapolis, 1978.

3. Mussan, P. and Eisenberg-Berg, N., *Roots of Caring, Sharing, and Helping*, W. H. Freeman, San Francisco, 1978.

4. Prutzman, P., Burger, M. L., Bodenhammer, G., and Stern, L., *The Friendly Classroom for a Small Planet*, Avery Publishing Group, New Jersey, 1978.

The middle years of schooling are equally, if not more, crucial for planet-conscious education. A comprehensive review of research into the socialization of children suggests that the period from age 7 to 12 is 'optimal both for education directed towards attitudinal objectives and for openness about the world. These five years are unique. They come before too many stereotypic attitudes dominate the child's view of the world, and are concurrent with the period in which the child's cognitive development is sufficiently advanced to accept a diversity of viewpoints'[41]. Students aged 7 to 12 have been found to be:

☐ intensely curious about the wider world in all its variety;

☐ particularly favourably disposed towards other cultures (with interest and toleration reaching a peak at 11–12);

☐ open and flexible in their attitudes to social and political issues;

☐ aware of, and interested in, issues to do with human rights[42].

A Rain Forest Project with 10–11 year olds

Elaine Hicks

Children need to develop a sense of wonder at the incredible variety, complexity and interdependence of the rainforest before they can begin to grasp what the consequences of its destruction would mean for the Earth's environment. My class of 10–11 year olds first brainstormed their ideas about rainforest. Stereotyped images of Tarzan, tribes and trees emerged alongside some total misconceptions (a rainforest, one student suggested, was a sandy beach with palm trees!). No-one appeared to have any idea of the interdependence of life in the rainforest and that this life was under threat.

To help the children to appreciate the beauty and richness of rainforest life, they watched a video presentation and looked at some colour photographs. They then set to work in pairs, drawing and writing down their immediate recollections of what they had seen. Further information was obtained from reference books and, later, the children wrote their own poems and reflections about life in the rainforest. These pieces of work showed a considerable gain in the childrens' understanding about rainforest ecology.

Next, to start the students thinking about the environmental issues of the equatorial forests, I used an activity pack for the 8–13 age range, published by Green Light Publications* – *A Rainforest Child*. The activities suggested were extremely useful in encouraging my class to think about and discuss how human beings use the rainforests and their products. The pack offers the activities as a means of informing children about why the forests are being destroyed. Lots of group discussion resulted.

It is at this point, when the children have come to an understanding about the whole fabric of rainforest life, that it is possible to begin considering what might be done to avert such destruction. Class work can here include asking children to think what they themselves can do; for this issue has serious implications for both their own future and the future of Planet Earth.

continued

Elaine Hicks teaches at Cabot Primary School, St. Paul's, Bristol.

* *A Rainforest Child. An Activity Based Teaching Pack*, Green Light Publications, Ty Bryn, Coombe Gardens, Llangynog, Carmarthen, Dyfed SA33 5AY.

Life in the jungle

Jungle has lots of trees
   So the light is dim.
Jungles have quick jaguars
   who catch fish.
Spiders' crafty webs catch out helpless bats.

Birds make nests
   But sneaky birds pinch them,
Nests are made from mud and twigs,
   Eggs are hatched,
But some birds are killed by worms inside.

Army ants, another creature, kills every thing
   That can't escape!
That's the life in the jungle.

by Simon Jackson, Cabot Primary School,
St. Pauls, Bristol.

With the onset of adolescence, there is a tendency towards withdrawal of sympathy, inflexibility and intolerance unless the opportunities presented by the middle school years for raising awareness of global issues and exploring attitudes have been used to good advantage. The World Studies 8–13 Project, which has now been implemented in primary and middle schools in some forty-five English and Welsh local education authorities, based its work on the research findings outlined above. Its major publication, *World Studies 8–13, A teachers handbook*[43], offers an exciting range of classroom activities.

Students' hopes and fears

We need to constantly remind ourselves that schooling only forms part of education. Even young children are daily bombarded with images of and information about major global problems whether on BBC television's John Craven's *Newsround* or other programmes. The hopes and fears such programmes raise, students bring with them to the classroom; teachers have a responsibility to allow the real concerns of those in their charge to be aired, discussed and investigated within a caring and concerned environment. Equally, teachers have a responsibility to ensure that students are not left with a sense of helplessness and hopelessness in the face of global problems. Ideas for action, and the practice of action skills, are crucial components of any effective programme.

A small-scale survey undertaken by the Centre for Global Education revealed that between eight and twenty per cent of children in top junior and first year secondary classes in a range of English schools watched the 1984 BBC late-evening television drama-documentary, Threads, *depicting a nuclear attack on Sheffield.*

Teenagers Talking[44]

Dear Beth,
Why is this called the happiest time of our life? I have a lot of worries and so do my friends. I don't just worry about dates and studies, I worry about other things going on in the world. Suppose there is a nuclear war. Suppose the air gets polluted. Suppose there isn't any gas left when I grow up, if I get to grow up at all. I wonder why we go to school and work so hard if it's all for nothing. Some of my friends do drugs and drink because they say they aren't going to last anyway, so why not? We're just kids and powerless to do anything about it. Did it always seem this way to teenagers?

– letter to an advice columnist

DEAR MR. PRESIDENT,

I KNOW YOU'RE PROBABLY PROUD OF MAN'S KNOWLEDGE BUT MAN'S KNOWLEDGE IS DESTROYING THE EARTH AND THE EARTH DOESN'T JUST BELONG TO MAN. IF WE GET INTO A WAR, I'M NOT JUST WORRIED ABOUT ME AND MY FAMILY OR PEOPLE. IF WE WANT TO DESTROY OURSELVES, WE SHOULD DO IT WITHOUT NATURE.

WHEN I THINK ABOUT THE WAY PEOPLE TREAT THE EARTH AND THE WAY ANIMALS TREAT THE EARTH, I FIND A BIG DIFFERENCE.

What are some of the principal concerns of students in Britain in the mid 1980s? A *Young Guardian* survey, conducted in October and November 1986, discovered that a national sample of 10–17 year-olds saw famine and poverty and nuclear war/weapons as the principal problems affecting the whole world whilst unemployment and nuclear war/weapons were regarded as the most serious national problems. Worries, the survey found, generally increased with age. A second survey conducted in August 1986 by MORI on behalf of the World Wildlife Fund asked children to list environmental and world problems they had heard about. Of the 243 children aged 6–10 questioned, 28% listed famine (18% referring specifically to Ethiopia), 12% crime, 10% the extinction of plants and animals, 9% pollution and 9% nuclear power. Of the 281 11–15 year olds questioned 33% mentioned pollution, 29% famine (11% referring specifically to Ethiopia), 23% crime, 22% nuclear power and 11% the extinction of plants and animals.

In 1983 thirty 9–10 year olds in an Oxfordshire primary class were invited to each write a list of questions they would like to ask about the future. Individual lists were to be compiled without any help from the teacher or friends. Finally, a composite class list was drawn up. The most frequently recurring questions on the individual lists were: will there be a nuclear war? (15 students), will nuclear weapons be abolished? (8 students), will there be an end to the world? (6 students) and will schools be the same? (6 students). Questions appearing more than once included: will we get worldwide pollution? will there still be poor people? will cars run on electricity? and will there be more old people's homes? The composite class questionnaire provided a basis for interview work with adults which formed part of a larger project on the future. One boy, subsequently reflecting on his hoped-for future, wrote:

'I would like to live in a world where there were not always wars going on somewhere and there were not always wars expected. I would like everybody to have the right amount of food and not some to have too little and others to have too much. I don't think its fair that some people die of hunger and others die or get ill because of too much food. I would like car exhausts to be made on the right rather than on the left because I always get a lot of smoke in my socks and they smell the day after. It is also dangerous for people to breathe in fumes[45].'

Research and experience show that children from a very early age are both fascinated and troubled by the future. Their fascination and worries are a proper concern of the professional teacher.

Subject-based approaches in the secondary school

Just as a systematic programme of planet-conscious education is required in the infant and junior school, so it is important across all subjects at secondary level. Here are some suggestions as to how a global perspective can be infused across the secondary curriculum.

Language and Communications

☐ development, environmental, peace and rights themes in world literature, e.g. Nigerian Dan Fulani's *The Price of Liberty*, Hodder & Stoughton, 1982, a novel about the sale of dangerous pesticides in the 'Third World' by unscrupulous companies, suitable for lower secondary students, or *One Hundred Years of Solitude* by Gabriel Garcia Marquez, Picador, 1978, which will offer senior secondary students a compelling insight into life and perspectives in a small town in South America;

From Portbridge to Ecuador and on to York

Richard Heery and Mike Pasternak

From Portbridge to Ecuador and on to York is a course we created in 1985. It is a sequential teaching unit aimed at first year secondary children and integrates English, Performing Arts and World Studies so as to present children with the opportunity to become actively involved in their own education. The programme lasts for one year during which time the children pass through various learning stages. 'Portrbridge' (the name given to the imaginary town we created when we ran the project for the first time) is the second stage; it presents a simulation of a community threatened by development, and here the choices the children make have significance but only limited repercussions. 'Ecuador' (the country in which our play was set when the project first ran) has the children devise a drama on an environmental subject. (To date rural depopulation in Ecuador and land erosion in Nepal have been tackled as the play topic.) Many of the choices here are their own but the teacher reserves the right to direct, sometimes

---

quite vigorously. 'York' is the final stage where the children from our school visit schools elsewhere (Yorkshire was the location in the first year of the project) to teach the children there and then jointly perform the play. The choices they make here are crucial. Throughout the course active learning processes are applied.

The following extract from the second stage of the programme shows how we included some of the ideas and concerns inherent in global education and education for environmental awareness.

Stage 2 – The First Choice

This section of the work consisted of a simulation type activity. The children take on identities within a community, the equilibrium of which is thrown into social turmoil by the introduction of a new factor (such as the planned development of a nuclear power station).

The following stages perhaps give some idea of the scope and range of activities.

1. The persona are created by the children themselves who:
    a. receive a card, empty except for a photograph;
    b. give this photograph a name, marital status and children;
    c. pass their cards on to another student who adds some personal characteristics;
    d. repass their cards for the addition of the character's most formative experience.

My name is Janet Sylvian Woolman, I am married and have divorced twice ... I have never really been interested in bringing up my own children ... I very often lose my temper when he's quite late in from work. I hate a lot of company ... My first husband died in a car accident.

2. The persona are developed through:
    a. games (of memory);
    b. improvisation;
    c. written autobiographies;

My name is John K. Gurtousixiy. I was born in 1961 on the 13th January in Mongolia but I am Irish. I have a nice quiet character. My early childhood up till university was uneventful. Just before entering university I took up skin diving until an incident put me off. One day I was diving I saw a tiger shark ... I surfaced to see that I was swimming in a sea of blood ... My hobbies are coins and shark teeth collecting ...

My name is Anne Jones and I am forty six years old ... I was born at the end of World War II in a bomb shelter ...

    d. collections of memorabilia;
    e. puppetry.

continued

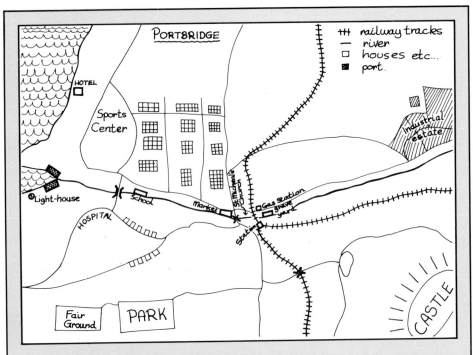

3. An environment evolves through:
  a. collaboration with the Geography department on authentic settlement patterns;
  b. library research on place names;
  c. the communal drawing, on a large piece of sugar paper, of the private houses, the public buildings and particular features of the settlement;
  d. three-dimensional modelling;
  e. individual maps.

4. The environment is threatened by the implications of the contents of an article in the imaginary local newspaper which:

  a. reveals the plans for some major public or private development (such as a nuclear power station);

PORTBRIDGE BUGLE
POWER STATION SHOCK

Reliable sources yesterday revealed that plans to build a nuclear power station in the area of Portbridge are well advanced. Until now the plans had been kept a closely guarded secret for fear that objectors to the scheme would prejudice the local population against it ...

  b. may be used for class discussion of reporting bias;

5. The people react to the news by:
   a. calling a public meeting;
   b. holding that meeting and formally proposing certain actions, such as
   c. inviting experts to give more information;
   d. writing letters to the newspaper;
   e. informal conversations, etc.

(We cannot be over-prescriptive because the essence of this part is spontaneous reaction.)

6. The class look to the future by presenting their individual views of the probable outcome of the situation as it evolved in Part 5 in the form of:

   a. dramatic presentations;
   b. newspaper articles;
   c. personal diaries;
   d. video films, etc.

Mike Pasternak is Head of Performing Arts and Richard Heery Head of English at the La Chataigneraie campus of the International School of Geneva.

☐ comprehension and writing, and the development of discussion skills, around global themes;

☐ the use of drama and role play to elucidate global issues and the different perspectives surrounding those issues;

☐ the study of Francophone Africa and Spanish-speaking Central and South America within French and Spanish classes;

☐ global issues through modern languages – an excellent textbook for the French Classroom is *Orientations*, Hodder & Stoughton, 1985, which includes lively discussion material on, amongst other themes, the Greenpeace protest about nuclear testing, Tanzanian coffee, colonialism and food production, women defending their rights in Chad and racist incidents in the Paris Metro;

☐ the role of France, Germany (or the national home of whichever language is being studied) in the world.

For other useful ideas see 'Language and Literature for understanding and transforming the World' which is World Studies Journal, Vol. 5, No. 3, 1984.

Humanities

- [ ] the historical development of global interdependencies (e.g. the development of the world trading system, the history of transnational corporations, case study histories of the work of U.N. development and environmental agencies);

- [ ] a thematic approach to history based on themes such as neo-colonialism, conflict/ conflict management, human rights and development;

- [ ] local history topics that help students understand how global trends, developments and events affect the lives of ordinary people;

- [ ] different meanings and models of development in geography (using materials which allow those with different perspectives to speak for themselves);

- [ ] the geography of environmental threats, global conflict and shortfalls in realizing human rights aspirations;

- [ ] drawing imaginary maps of the future in the light of current social, political, economic and environmental trends;

- [ ] religious perspectives on development and environment (see, for instance, the World Wildlife Fund's *Worlds of difference* pack);

- [ ] the global economic system and its effects on developed and underdeveloped countries;

- [ ] the economic effects of environmental problems.

Development and environmental issues through mathematics

Brian Hudson

'Mathematics lessons in schools are very often not about anything,' declared the influential Cockcroft Report on the teaching of mathematics. More effective mathematics teaching, the Report urged, would follow if students were asked to make use of 'real life' data rather than data which had been artificially contrived. Development and environmental issues offer 'real life' data in abundance. Such issues can be highlighted by devising activities or units of work which draw upon relevant global statistics. The following classroom activity is one example of the type of approach that mathematics teachers can adopt to meet the twofold aim of developing mathematical skills and concepts and developing a concerned awareness of global issues.

The statistics in the tables below are from a data base designed for use in the mathematics classroom. The left-hand column of figures in each table deals with average life expectancy – less than fifty years in Table A and greater than seventy two years in Table B (1983 figures). The data base is used in conjunction with the information retrieval program QUESTD. The right-hand column in each table records the percentage of population with access to safe water.

Table A

COUNTRY	LIFE EXPEC	WATER
OMAN	49	52%
YEMEN, ARAB REPUBLIC	43	4%
YEMEN, PEOPLES DEMOCRATIC REPUBLIC	46	37%
AFGHANISTAN	37	10%
BANGLADESH	48	68%
NEPAL	45	11%
LAOS	43	48%
ANGOLA	42	17%
BURUNDI	45	
CENTRAL AFRICAN REP.	43	18%
CHAD	43	26%
CONGO	43	26%
ETHIOPIA	46	13%
GUINEA	43	10%
IVORY COAST	47	14%
MADAGASCAR	48	26%
MALAWI	44	44%
MALI	45	23%
MAURITANIA	44	17%
MOZAMBIQUE	49	7%
NIGER	45	49%
NIGERIA	49	28%
RWANDA	46	38%
SENEGAL	44	35%
SIERRA LEONE	47	9%
SOMALIA	39	38%
SUDAN	47	46%
TOGO	48	11%
UGANDA	48	16%
BURKINA FASO	44	14%
KAMPUCHEA	39	45%

Table B

COUNTRY	LIFE EXPEC	WATER
UNITED STATES	75	99%
CANADA	75	99%
CUBA	73	62%
BELGIUM	73	89%
DENMARK	75	99%
FRANCE	76	97%
WEST GERMANY	73	99%
GREECE	74	97%
ITALY	74	86%
NETHERLANDS	76	97%
NORWAY	76	98%
UNITED KINGDOM	74	99%
BULGARIA	73	
EAST GERMANY	73	82%
POLAND	73	55%
AUSTRIA	73	88%
FINLAND	75	84%
SPAIN	74	78%
IRELAND	73	73%
SWEDEN	77	99%
SWITZERLAND	76	96%
ISRAEL	73	99%
JAPAN	77	98%
AUSTRALIA	74	97%
NEW ZEALAND	74	93%
COSTA RICA	73	81%

The information may be investigated in a systematic way by drawing a scatter diagram as illustrated below – a line of positive slope indicating a direct correlation. Statistics on the remaining countries covered in the data base (127 in all) would obviously complete the picture.

continued

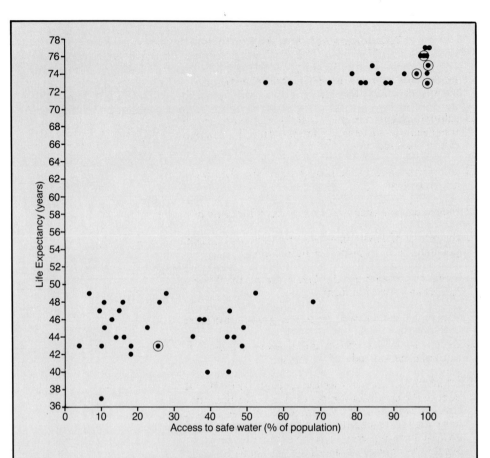

This theme can be developed further by looking at statistics related to energy, resource depletion, soil erosion and hence, problems of drought. Such activities offer practice in statistics whilst at the same time providing a springboard for discussion of, and possibly enquiry into, key world problems. As one mathematics teacher in an inner-city multi-ethnic comprehensive school who used the data base put it: 'it offered an original and interesting approach to statistics and aided pupils' personal development in their awareness of world problems'.

The data base, *Global Statistics*, offers 20 pieces of information (others include population, GNP, military expenditure and literacy rates) on each of the 127 countries. It is available, with an accompanying teaching package for the mathematics classroom called *Global Problems*, from the Centre for Global Education, York University.

Brian Hudson, formerly Head of Mathematics at Greenlands High School for Girls, Blackpool, is now Senior Lecturer in Mathematics Education at the Mathematics Education Centre, Sheffield City Polytechnic.

Science and Maths

☐ global statistics as raw material for developing numeracy and statistical skills;

☐ cultural achievement and diversity as exemplified in the counting systems, geometry, etc., of different cultures and societies;

☐ studying ecosystems, habitats, energy flow, food webs, etc., in biology;

☐ the biology and chemistry of the Green Revolution;

☐ the effects of environmental/development decisions, pollutants, etc., on plant and animal life;

☐ comparative study of the behaviour of the human species and other life forms;

☐ the physics and chemistry of recycling waste materials;

☐ the environmental impact and development implications of chemical/industrial processes;

☐ 'Third World' science – see the excellent Third World Science Project Packs, illustrating basic scientific principles at work in 'Third World' contexts; titles include 'Carrying loads on heads', 'Distillation', 'Fermentation' and 'Methane digesters', (available from the Centre for World Development Education, see page 83).

For other useful ideas see 'Global Pi: world studies in the science and maths classroom', World Studies Journal, Vol. 5, No. 4, 1985.

Global Perspective in Chemistry Teaching

Patrick Hazlewood

The infusion of global perspectives into secondary school chemistry emerges from the premise that no curriculum subject is an island. The lives of people, the development of human communities, the care of Planet Earth and the need for every individual to *think* about the future can all be incorporated into the study of chemistry. Chemistry itself has a vital contribution to make to a real understanding of these issues.

If we see the Earth as comprising several vital categories of resource, then

continued

a close relationship between development and environmental issues, on the one hand, and chemistry, on the other, emerges. Metals, Energy, the Air and Nitrogen, for instance, are topics that encompass the fundamental resource demands that humankind makes on the environment. Again, if we take the concept of environmental pollution, a wide variety of possible points of focus emerge – such as acid rain, dioxins, by-products of metal extraction, by-products of petro-chemical industries and non-recyclable plastics. All are essentially chemical in origin. But where, some might wonder, does the boundary of chemistry end and the need for educated and informed citizens begin?

Chemistry is not an isolationist educational discipline. Studying the environmental effects of bauxite extraction is not as straightforward as a spoil heap obstructing scenic views; nor is it as simple as quarrying noise levels or transportational pollution. In studying simple aluminium chemistry, basic experiments are used to place Al in the reactivity series. Reactions of metals with acids, placing metals in solutions of their salts, the thermite reaction all point to the position in the series, but it is clearly unusual in that it doesn't seem to behave the way it should. Discussion about why it appears unreactive follows on naturally and further investigation suggest reasons why Al is so important to Western civilization. In nature Al is no less difficult to extract from its ore and this is the beginning of a complex web. Energy in vast quantities is required for the purification of aluminium. Where

continued

does it come from? In the case of Malaysia, the Bakun Dam Project, Sarawak, is a typical example of issues which chemistry cannot forget and must *not* ignore. Nearly 400 km^2 of rainforest will be submerged to provide the reservoir; the Malaysian people will need to finance the project to the tune of M$40 billion, which can never be repaid in the dam's forty-year life-span. So who will use the hydro-electric power produced by the dam? Only 4% will be used by the Malay people – the other 90+% will be used by multinational companies such as the proposed Reynold's Aluminium Smelter in Bintulu. It seems, therefore, that the economic and natural resources of a relatively under-developed country are again being exploited by Western countries.

Direct pressures on the local inhabitants in terms of economic debt are considerable even if offset a little by limited employment spin-offs. However, the potential contribution of the project to global disaster, in terms of increased carbon dioxide build up in the atmosphere and hence gradual increase in the earth's temperature, is frightening. The destruction of rainforests has consequences for all inhabitants of the earth, human and otherwise. On a local level again, the relatively still waters provide ideal breeding grounds for malarial mosquitoes; geophysicists fear a dramatically increased likelihood of earthquakes because of the weight of water on geological fault lines.

Clearly, an extractive chemical process is not as straightforward as it appears. Economic, political, scientific, environmental, developmental and humanitarian issues are closely linked with geographical, physical and chemical factors. This example is by no means isolated – it is the tip of a huge iceberg which incorporates gold mining and apartheid in South Africa, mineral exploitation and devastation of the Amazonian rainforests, famine in Ethiopia, nuclear power issues, acid rain ...

Chemistry in the laboratory is one important key to an understanding of global issues. More than that, it is one way of educating our children about the world around them that will enable them to help the world tomorrow.

Patrick Hazlewood is Head of Science at The Queen's School, Wisbech, Cambridgeshire.

The Arts, Design and Recreation

☐ art as a means of helping children to look at the environment and, through looking and drawing, to develop their imaginative, emotional and sensory capacities – see Bev Joicey, *An Eye on the Environment: an Art Education Project*, Bell & Hyman/ World Wildlife Fund, 1986;

☐ creative art, design and music work around global themes and images of the future (e.g. students are given stimulus material on a theme and form groups to compose, practise and perform songs responding to the theme) – see 'Art in Action' *World Studies Journal*, Vol. 5, No. 1, 1984, for useful ideas;

☐ music as a stimulus for student reflection on social, political, economic and environmental problems – see for instance the World Wildlife Fund's *Yanomamo* and *African Jigsaw*;

☐ the point of origin of goods, clothes, fabrics, furniture, etc., used in the home or for sport and recreation;

☐ the environmental implications of foods and materials found in the home, e.g. beefburgers, mahogany tables;

☐ co-operative sports and games – see Tom Schneider's *Everybody's a winner*, Little, Brown and Co., Toronto, 1976, and Terry Orlick's *The Co-operative Sports and Games Book*, Writers and Readers, 1982.

Where we stand!

Positional Statements from Those of Influence in the World of Education

Reasonable Expectations by Age 16.
It seems important that those who will shortly become autonomous citizens should, to the extent of their capacities:

a. view their surroundings with an eye both appreciative and critical;
b. be competent in a range of environmentally-related skills;
c. understand something of the processes of the physical world, and especially have a basic knowledge of ecological principles and relationships;
d. understand something of the economic, technological, planning and political processes which affect man's use of the environment.
e. have a degree of insight into other peoples' environments, life-styles and predicaments;
f. understand something of the interdependence of peoples and the nature of the resource-base upon which mankind relies;
g. show developing attitudes of concern towards their environment and the environment of others;
h. in so far as environmental issues are concerned, have a basis on which to develop the ability to make informed decisions affecting themselves and society – and the interest to do so.

– HMI, *Curriculum 11–16*, Department of Education and Science, 1977.

Many of the areas covered by peace education will overlap with the 'family' of studies which includes multicultural, environmental and development education and world studies. The Union believes that these fields should not be seen as competing for timetable space but rather as offering different, often complementary approaches.

– NUT, *Education for Peace*, 1984.

The ultimate aims of environmental education are the creation of responsible attitudes and the development of an environmental ethic.

– HM Inspectors of Schools for the Scottish Education Department, 1974.

We live in a complex, interdependent world and many of our problems in Britain require international solutions. The curriculum should therefore reflect our need to know more about and understand other countries.
– Department of Education and Science, *Education in Schools: a Consultative Document*, 1977.

A good knowledge must in our view give every youngster the knowledge, understanding and skills to function effectively as an individual, as a citizen of the wider national society in which he lives and in the interdependent world community of which he is also a member.

– Swann Committee, *Education for All*, 1985.

We call on leaders of public opinion, on educators, on all interested bodies to contribute to an increased public awareness of both the origins and the severity of the critical situation facing mankind today.

Everybody has the right to understand fully the nature of the systems of which he is a part, as a producer, as a consumer, as one among the billions populating the earth. He has the right to know who benefits from the fruits of his work, who benefits from what he buys and sells, and the degree to which he enhances or degrades his planetary inheritance.

A United Nations Meeting, Mexico, 1974.

International tensions, the continuing expansion of nuclear and conventional armaments, and the negative response of the developed nations to the needs of the Third World ... all demonstrate the relevance and indeed urgent importance of peace education as part of an overall strategy for the elimination of conflict and the reallocation of resources.

– NUT/NATFHE, *Education for Peace*, 1981.

Learning for Living means growing up learning to take responsibility for one's own learning and the quality of one's environment, with an increasing awareness of obligations to others and to the natural world. A constructive environmental policy backed by a balanced educational programme aimed to foster environmental competence, to identify the health of one's environment with one's own health, to encourage national participation in the development for all of a sustainable life-style, for the future as well as for the present, this is the policy we must continue to work for.

– Scottish Environmental Education Council, *Learning for Living*, 1985.

Suggested aims for schools:

(i)   to help pupils to develop lively, enquiring minds, the ability to question and argue rationally and to apply themselves to tasks, and physical skills;

(ii) to help pupils *to acquire knowledge and skills relevant to adult life and employment in a fast changing world*;

(iii) to help pupils to use language and number effectively;

(iv) *to instill respect for religious and moral values, and tolerance of other races, religions and ways of life*;

(v)   *to help pupils to understand the world in which they live, and the interdependence of individuals, groups and nations.*

– A *Framework for the School Curriculum*, Department of Education and Science, 1980 (our italics)

Ten Starting Points for Teachers

1. Contact and/or join the following organisations for information about networks, other people working in the field, events, resources etc: Centre for Global Education, University of York, Heslington, York, YO1 5DD. Tel: 0904 413267; Council for Education in World Citizenship, Seymour Mews House, Seymour House, Seymour Mews, London W1H 9PE. Tel: 01-935 1752; Council for Environmental Education, School of Education, University of Reading, London Road, Reading RG1 5AQ. Tel: 0734 875234 Ext. 218; Council of Europe Human Rights in Education Group (U.K.), c/o British Institute of Human Rights, Kings College, Strand, London WC2R 2LS; National Association of Development Education Centres, 6 Endsleigh Street, London, WC1H 0DX. Tel: 01-388 2670; National Association for Environmental Education, West Midlands College of Higher Education, Gorway, Walsall, WS1 3BD; Peace Education Network, Centre for Peace Studies, St. Martin's College, Bowerham, Lancaster LA1 3JD. Tel: 0524 37698; Scottish Environmental Education Council, c/o Biology Dept., Paisley College, High Street, Paisley PA1 2BE.

2. For background reading on the ideas and philosophy outlined in this booklet: Allen, R., *How to Save the World*, Kogan Page, 1980; Caldecott, L. & Leland, S., (eds.) *Reclaim the Earth*, The Women's Press, 1983; Capra, F., *The Turning Point*, Fontana, 1983; Ferguson, M., *The Aquarian Conspiracy*, Paladin, 1982; Houston, J., *The Possible Human*, J. P. Tarcher, Los Angeles, 1982; Porritt, J., *Seeing Green*, Blackwell, 1984; Robertson, J., *The Sane Alternative*, James Robertson (Spring Cottage, 9 New Road, Ironbridge, Shropshire TF8 7AU), 1983; Roszak, T., *Person/Planet*, Granada, 1981.

3. For background data on environmental, development, peace and rights issues: Grant, J. P., *State of the World's Children*, Oxford University Press, 1987; Kidron, M. and Segal, R., *The New State of the World Atlas*, Pan, 1984; Myers, N., (ed.) *The Gaia Atlas of Planet Management*, Pan, 1985; Seager, J. and Olson, A., *Women in the World – an international atlas*, Pan, 1986; Sivard, R. L., *World Military and Social Expenditures* 1983, World Priorities, Washington, 1983; *World Bank Atlas*, The World

Bank, Washington, (publ. every year); *World Development Report*, The World Bank, Washington, (publ. every year); World Resources Institute/International Institute for Environment and Development, *World Resources 1986*, Basic Books, 1986.

4. Subscribe to the following journals: *Action for Development*, Centre for World Development Education, Regent's College, Inner Circle, Regent's Park, London NW1 4NS; *Bulletin of Environmental Education*, c/o Notting Dale Urban Studies Centre, 189 Freston Road, London W10 6TH; *Contemporary Issues in Geography and Education*, Geography Department, London University Institute of Education, 20 Bedford Way, London, WC1; *Environmental Education*, National Association for Environmental Education, West Midlands College of Higher Education, Gorway, Walsall, WS1 3BD; *Green Teacher*, Llys Awel, 22 Heol Pentrerhedyn, Machynlleth, Powys, SY20 8DN; *The New Era*, The Institute of Education, University of London, London, WC1H 0LA: *New Internationalist*, 42 Hythe Bridge Street, Oxford, OX1 2EP; *REED*, Council for Environmental Education, School of Education, University of Reading, London Road, Reading RG1 5AQ; *World Studies Journal*, Centre for Global Education, University of York, Heslington, York, YO1 5DD.

5. For lists of organisations look at the following directories: *Directory for the Environment: Organisations in Britain and Ireland 1984–5* Routledge and Kegan Paul, 1984; *Education for Peace – Resource Guide* Westbourne Teachers' Centre, 17 Westbourne Road, Sheffield S10 2QQ, 1984; *Environmental Education Enquiries*, Conservation Trust, George Palmer Site, Northumberland Avenue, Reading, Berks RG2 7PW, 1986; *Environmental Education; Sources of Information*, D.E.S., 1981; *Overseas development and aid: A Guide to sources of information and material*, O.D.A., 1986; *World Studies Resources Guide*, C.E.W.C., 1984.

See, also, the *List of Human Rights Organisations* published by the Centre for Global Education (Global Education Documentation Service, No. 19).

6. In-service training opportunities are afforded by: the bi-annual conference of the World Studies Network (c/o Hugh Starkey, Westminster College, North Hinksey, Oxford OX2 9AT); the regular conferences organised by the World Studies 8–13 Project (c/o David Hicks, Centre for Peace Studies, St Martin's

College, Lancaster LA1 3JD); the Diploma courses, conferences, workshops and in-school/in-LEA consultancies offered by the Centre for Global Education (University of York, Heslington, York YO1 5DD); the local courses run by Development Education Centres (see 10 below) and Department of Education and Science short and long courses (the programmes for short and long courses are available from HMI Support Services, DES, Elizabeth House, 37 York Road, London SE1 7PH). Forthcoming in-service events are regularly featured in the Centre for Global Education's termly *Global Education News*.

7. For information about classroom resources obtain the educational catalogues of the Centre for World Development Education (see 4 above), Christian Aid (P.O. Box No. 1, London SW9 8BH) and Oxfam Youth and Education Department, 274 Banbury Road, Oxford OX2 7DZ. Other extremely useful publications are: *Goldmine Resources for Teachers*, David Brown, P.O. Box 82, Seaford, Sussex BN25 2JF: *Switching on to the Environment: A critical guide to films on environment and development*, Television Trust for the Environment; *Materials for Teachers*, World Wildlife Fund, 11–13 Ockford Road, Godalming, Surrey GU7 1QU; *Teaching Resources for Education in International Understanding, Justice and Peace*, Marc Goldstein Memorial Trust, University of London Institute of Education. For excellent 16mm film and video material, contact Concord Films Council, 201 Felixstowe Road, Ipswich, Suffolk IP3 9BJ (annual catalogue available) and the International Broadcasting Trust, 2 Ferdinand Place, London NW1 8EE.

8. For ideas on classroom activities see the following practical handbooks: Borba, M. and Borba, C., *Self Esteem: A Classroom Affair; Vol. I*, Winston Press, Minneapolis, 1978; *Vol. 2*, Harper and Row, San Francisco, 1982; Braun, D. and Pearson, J., *Priorities for Development*, Development Education Centre, Gillet Centre, Selly Oak Colleges, Bristol Road, Birmingham, B29 6LE, 1982; Fisher, S. and Hicks, D., *World Studies 8–13*, Oliver and Boyd, 1985; Fyson, N. L., *The Development Puzzle*, Hodder and Stoughton, 1984; Judson, S., (ed.) *A Manual on Nonviolence and Children*, New Society, Philadelphia, 1977, Pike, G. and Selby D., *Global Teacher, Global Learner*, Hodder & Stoughton, 1987; Prutzman, P. *et al. The Friendly Classroom for a Small Planet*, Avery, New Jersey, 1978; Masheder, M., *Let's Co-operate*, Peace Education Project, 1986; World Studies Project,

Learning for Change in World Society, World Studies Project, 1979.

Borba and Borba, Judson, Prutzman and Masheder are particularly useful for the infant and junior classroom.

9. Simulations and role-playing exercises are particularly useful techniques when dealing with environmental, development, peace and rights issues. The following organisations or publications are good sources of material: Centre for Global Education, University of York, Heslington, York, YO1 5DD. Tel: 0904 413267 (e.g. *Timber!*); Centre for World Development Education, Regent's College, Inner Circle, Regent's Park, London, NW1 4NS. Tel: 01-487 5438 (e.g. *Sand Harvest* – computer simulation on Sahel); Christian Aid, PO Box 1, London, SW9 8BH. Tel: 01-733 5500 (e.g. *Trading Game*); Community Service Volunteers, 237 Pentonville Road, London, N1 9NJ. Tel: 01-278 6601 (e.g. *Spring Green Motorway*); Oxfam Youth and Education Department, 274 Banbury Road, Oxford, OX2 7DZ. Tel: 0865 56777 (e.g. *Panchayat*). *Intercom* No. 75 'Teaching Global Issues through Simulation' and No. 107 'Simulations for a Global Perspective' are available from the Centre for Global Education. Also for further reading: Davison and Gordon, *Games and Simulations in Action*, Woburn Press, 1978; Jones, K., *Designing your own simulations*, Methuen, 1985.

10. For action, whether in terms of fieldwork, fund-raising or campaigning, contact the following for information about local groups: Contact British Trust for Conservation Volunteers, Schools Officer, Conservation Centre, Firsby Road, Quinton, Birmingham B32 2QT, for details of its network of local groups which carry out and give advice on practical conservation work (BTCV also administer a grant scheme to schools for such work); Fairbrother Group, c/o Landlife, 25 Gerrard Street, Lancaster, for a list of local urban conservation groups/study centres; Architecture Workshops, RIBA, 66 Portland Place, London W1N 4AD, for a list of local architecture workshops; NADEC for a list of local Development Education Centres; WATCH Trust for Environmental Education, 22 The Green, Nettleham, Lincoln LN2 2NR, for details of local WATCH groups.

Other organisations (by no means an exhaustive list!) engaged in campaigning activities on development, environmental, rights and peace issues are: Amnesty International, 1 Easton Street, London, WC1X 8DJ;

Community Service Volunteers, 237 Pentonville Road, London, N1 9NJ; Friends of the Earth, 377 City Road, London, EC1V 1NA; Greenpeace, 36 Graham Street, London, N1 8LL; International Voluntary Service, Ceresole House, 53 Regent Road, Leicester, LE1 67L; International Year of Shelter for the Homeless, 19–29 Woburn Place, London, WC1H 0LY; Oxfam – Hungry for Change, (see 7 above); World Development Movement, Bedford Chambers, Covent Garden, London, WC2E 8HA.

References

1. World Resources Institute International Institute for Environment and Development, *World Resources 1986*, Basic Books, New York, 1986.

2. Myers, N., (ed.) *The Gaia Atlas of Planet Management*, Pan Books, 1985.

3. Houston, J., *The Possible Human*, J. P. Tarcher, Los Angeles, 1982.

4. Capra, F., *The Turning Point: Science, society and the rising culture*, Fontana, 1983.

5. Myers, N., in *The Guardian*, 26 February 1987.

6. Schumacher, E. F., *Small is Beautiful*, Abacus, 1974.

7. *The Global 2000 Report to the President*, Penguin, 1981.

8. Porritt, J., *Seeing Green: The Politics of Ecology Explained*, Blackwell, 1984.

9. Earth Resources Research, *Waste Recycling*, Information Sheet 5.

10. Hall, N., *The Moon and the Virgin*, The Womens Press, 1980.

11. Graham, A., *The Other Economic Summit*. 1984.

12. Central Statistical Office, *Social Trends* 15 H.M.S.O., 1985.

13. Sivard, R. L., *World Military and Social Expenditures 1983*, World Priorities, 1983.

14. U.N. Centre for Disarmament 'The Relationship between Disarmament and Development', Disarmament Study Series 5, A/36/356, New York, 1982.

15. *New Internationalist*, No. 121, March 1983.

16. Development Alternatives with Women for a New Era (DAWN), *Development, Crises, and Alternative Visions: Third World Women's Perspectives*, DAWN, 1985.

17. Higgins, R., *The Seventh Enemy: The Human Factor in the Global Crisis*, Hodder and Stoughton, 1982.

18. Meadows, D. C., Randers, D. H., and Behrens, W. W. *The Limits to Growth*, Pan, 1972.

19. Redclift, M., *Development and the Environmental Crisis: Red or Green Alternatives?*, Methuen, 1984.

20. Brandt Commission, *North–South: a programme for survival*, Pan, 1980.

21. Brandt Commission, *Common Crisis*, Pan, 1983.

22. I.U.C.N., *World Conservation Strategy*, I.U.C.N., 1980.

23. The Final Report of the Brundtland Commission is to be published in April, 1987.

24. Elgin, D., *Voluntary Simplicity*, Morrow & Co., New York, 1981.

25. Macey, J. R., *Despair and Personal Power in the Nuclear Age*, New Society Philadelphia, 1983.

26. Evans and Fraser Evans (eds.) *Human Rights: a Dialogue between First and Third Worlds*, Lutterworth Press, 1983.

27. Curle, A., 'The Scope and Dilemmas of Peace Studies', *Teaching Politics*, vol. 6, no. 3, 1977, cited in Brown, C., Harben, C., and Stevens, J., *Social Education: Principles and Practice*, Falmer Press, 1986.

28. Slaughter, R., 'The Dinosaur and The dream: Re-Thinking Education for the Future', *World Studies Journal*, Vol. 6, no. 1, 1985.

29. Roszak, T., *Unfinished Animal*, Faber & Faber, 1976.

30. Van Matre, S., *Acclimatization*, American Camping Association, Martinsville, Indiana, 1972; Van Matre, S., *Sunship Earth*, American Camping Association, 1979.

31. Roszak, T., *Person/Planet*, Granada, 1978.

32. See, for example, the research findings of Aspy & Roebuck and Tausch & Tausch in Rogers, C., *Freedom to learn for the 80s*, Merrill, Ohio, 1983.

33. Johnson, D. W., and Johnson R. T., 'The socialisation and achievement crisis: are co-operative learning experiences the solution?', in Bickman, L., (ed.), *Applied social psychology annual 4*, Sage Publications, 1983.

34. Rogers, C., *op. cit.*

35. Shirman, D., Conrad, D., 'Awareness, understanding and action: a global conscience in the classroom', *The New Era*, vol. 58, no. 6, December 1977.

36. Starkey, H., 'Human Rights: the values for world studies and multicultural education', Westminster Studies in Education, vol. 9, 1986.

37. Prutzman, P., et al., The Friendly Classroom for a Small Planet, Avery, New Jersey, 1978; Borba, M., and Borba, C., Self-Esteem: A Classroom Affair, Winston Press, Minneapolis, 1978; Mussen, P., and Eisenberg-Berg, N., Roots of Caring, Sharing, and Helping, Freeman, San Francisco, 1977.

38. Mussen, P., and Eisenberg-Berg, N., op. cit.; Spivack, G., and Shure, M., Social Adjustment of Young Children, Jossey-Bass, San Francisco.

39. Fountain, S., Affirmation, Communication, and Co-operation Experiences in an early Childhood Program, Diploma in Applied Educational Studies thesis, University of York, 1987.

40. Prutzman, P., et. al., op. cit.

41. Torney, J. V., 'Middle Childhood and International Education', Intercom, Centre for War/Peace Studies, New York, November 1972.

42. See, for instance, Buergenthal, T., and Torney, J. V., International Human Rights and International Education, U.S. National Commission for UNESCO, 1976, chap. 6; Torney-Purta, J. V., 'Socialization and Human Rights Research: Implications for Teachers' in Stimman Branson, M., and Torney-Purta, J. V., (eds.), International Human Rights, Society and the Schools, National Council for the Social Studies, Washington, Bulletin no. 68, 1982; Ross, A., 'Human Rights Education: Perspectives and Problems in the Primary School', World Studies Journal, vol. 2, no. 3, 1981.

43. Fisher, S., and Hicks, D. W., World Studies 8–13. A Teachers Handbook, Oliver & Boyd, 1984.

44. These quotations are cited in Van Ornum, W., and M. W., Talking to Children about Nuclear War, Continuum, New York, 1984.

45. Holden, C., 'Teaching about the Future with Younger Children: More than Space Ships and Battle Stars', World Studies Journal, vol. 6, no. 1, 1985.

Acknowledgements

Photography
Amanda Wood: 48
Associated press: 5
Bruce Coleman Ltd: 9, 18 above, 64
Bärbel Selby: 29 insert
Mr. Fairbrother: 76, 77
Helen Tann: VI
Jeremy Hartley: 12
Judah Passow: 29 insert
Losehill Hall: 42 above, 42 below
Mark Edwards: 2 centre, 15
Network Photographers: IV above, 11, 29 insert
NFSS: 42 above, 42 below
Oxfam: V below, V above, 2 above, 2 below, 18, 29
    insert, 29 insert
Panos Pictures: IV below, 15
Patrick Hazlewood: 76, 77
Susan Fountain: 61
Vic Fowler: 53
WWF: IV centre